DEAR _____

I BOUGHT YOU THIS BOOK BECAUSE:

- [ ] I saw the word 'stupid' and immediately thought of you
- [ ] It's new out and I know how you like to be 'with it'
- [ ] It was getting late and I had to buy you something
- [ ] I know how much you like reading in the toilet and this seemed ideal
- [ ] It didn't need much wrapping paper
- [ ] I thought it would appeal to your warped sense of humour
- [ ] I went into the bookshop to get out of the rain and happened to see it while I was pretending to browse
- [ ] You don't warrant a present costing any more than this
- [ ] They ran out of copies of _Sex Tips for the Useless_
- [ ] I wanted to read it myself first
- [ ] I'm one of the authors, and I got it at the wholesale price

7 Other Stupid Books by the Same Authors

✗ *The Complete Revenge Kit*
✗ *How to Be a Complete Bastard* (with Adrian Edmondson)
✗ *How to Be a Complete Bitch* (with Pamela Stephenson)
✗ *The Book of Revelations*
✗ *The Naughty 90s*
✗ *The Return of the Complete Revenge Kit*
✗ *How to Be a Superhero*

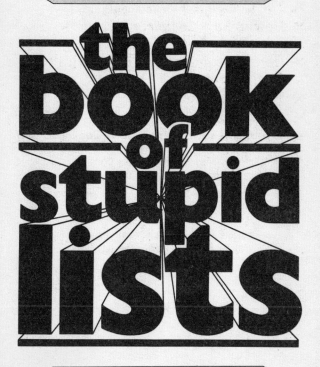

the book of stupid lists

Mike Lepine and Mark Leigh

VIRGIN

First published in Great Britain in 1991 by
Virgin Books
an imprint of Virgin Publishing Ltd
338 Ladbroke Grove
London W10 5AH

ISBN 0 86369 5388

Phototypeset by Intype, London

Printed and bound in Great Britain by
Cox & Wyman Ltd, Reading, Berks.

CONTENTS

25 Stupid People Who Have Helped Us with This Book

- Glen Cardno
- Terry Carter
- John Choopani
- Chris Fordwoh
- Paul Forty
- Harrie Green
- Melanie Hammerton
- Mary Hatton
- Philippa Hatton
- Sara Howell
- Ashley Kopitko
- Neville Landau
- Adam Leigh
- Debbie Leigh
- Edith Leigh
- Philip Leigh
- Alec Lepine
- Eileen Lepine
- Jo Marchment
- Miriam Markham
- Steven Markham
- James Ruppert
- Andrea Scott
- Tim Scott
- Rob Shreeve

OUR FURRY FRIENDS

14 Animals with Stupid Names

- Ocelot
- Aardvark
- Okapi
- Tapir
- Sperm whale
- Orang-utan
- Bandicoot
- Caribou
- Gecko
- Gnu
- Aye-aye
- Dingo
- Cuttlefish
- Ring-tailed lemur

---

5 Birds' Names That Raise a Snigger

- ◆ Blue Tit
- ◆ Coal Tit
- ◆ Great Tit
- ◆ Long-tailed Tit
- ◆ Greater Spotted Arsehole

---

11 Dogs That Look as Stupid as Their Names Sound

- ☆ Shar-pei
- ☆ Chow-chow
- ☆ Dachshund
- ☆ Chihuahua
- ☆ Lasa apso
- ☆ German spitz
- ☆ Pomeranian
- ☆ Samoyed
- ☆ Pug
- ☆ Schnauzer
- ☆ Shih-tzu

5 Stupid Birds That Can't Fly

- Ostrich
- Kiwi
- Emu
- Penguin
- Dead pigeon

12 Sandwich Fillings for People Who Like the Taste of Insects

- Cockroach and cress
- Mosquito and egg salad
- Weevil and tuna
- Flea and coleslaw
- Bluebottle and prawns
- Bumblebee and tomato
- Dung beetle and cheese
- Red ant and salmon paté
- Dragonfly and Branston pickle
- Earwig and coronation chicken
- Greenfly and lettuce
- Daddy-longlegs and ham on brown bread

10 Pop Stars or Groups Named After Creepy-Crawlies

- Adam and the Ants
- Ziggy Stardust and the Spiders from Mars
- The Beatles
- Sting
- The Ladybirds
- Buddy Holly and the Crickets
- Roachford
- The Scorpions
- Frank Zappa and the Moth-ers of Invention
- The Po-lice

12 Stupid Things to Try to Train Your Dog to Do

- ✕ Handstands
- ✕ Mechanical engineering
- ✕ Write its name
- ✕ Fetch a big bar of chocolate without eating it
- ✕ Fly a microlite
- ✕ Fly
- ✕ Practise safe sex
- ✕ Say Grace before eating
- ✕ Climb trees
- ✕ Complete complex jigsaw puzzles
- ✕ Play hopscotch with you
- ✕ Anything he doesn't want to do, basically

10 Stupid Reasons Why the Dinosaurs May Have Died Out

☛ They contracted 'mad dinosaur disease'

☛ Prince Philip's ancestors thought it was a 'topping wheeze' to hunt them for sport

☛ They all became gay

☛ They didn't watch their cholesterol levels

☛ They didn't fancy each other

☛ The Japanese were responsible

☛ They got hold of a sex instruction manual entitled *Great Sex the Giant Panda Way!*

☛ They worked too hard, ate too many fatty foods and spent too much time in front of the television set

☛ They smoked sixty a day

☛ They lived near a primitive nuclear power station and all the baby dinosaurs got leukaemia

10 Fairly Sure Signs That Someone Owns a Pit Bull Terrier

◆ They may not be able to count up to ten on their fingers (for one of two reasons)

◆ They have very small willies (also for one of two reasons)

◆ They've got a car window sticker showing a dog's head and the slogan 'Go on, break in – make his day!'

◆ There are police marksmen on the roof opposite their house

- They're on *News at Ten*, trying to shield their faces from the camera
- The postman throws their letters into the garden and then runs for it
- They very rarely get any visitors
- They have a swastika tattooed on their forehead
- You hear them running down the street at 3 a.m. yelling 'Genghis, come back with Wayne! Drop, boy, drop!'
- You hear them running down the street at 3.02 a.m. yelling ''Kin 'ell! 'Kin 'ell! It's gone mental!'

10 Animals That the Quick Brown Fox Jumped Over, Apart from the Lazy Dog

☆ The lethargic hedgehog

☆ The idle badger

☆ The slothful tortoise

☆ The indolent cat

☆ The workshy fieldmouse

☆ The languid weasel

☆ The inert vole

☆ The sluggish rabbit

☆ The torpid mole

☆ The inactive squirrel

13 Movies with Armadillos in Them

🎗 *Carry On Armadillo* (1964)

🎗 *Enter the Armadillo* (1973)

🎗 *The Day the Armadillo Stood Still* (1951)

✗ *Armadillo Day Afternoon* (1976)
✗ *All the President's Armadillos* (1976)
✗ *Gentlemen Prefer Armadillos* (1953)
✗ *A Clockwork Armadillo* (1971)
✗ *Gone with the Armadillo* (1939)
✗ *Butch Cassidy and the Sundance Armadillo* (1969)
✗ *The Silence of the Armadillos* (1991)
✗ *Armadillo* (1976)
✗ *Armadillo II* (1978)
✗ *Armadillo III* (1981)

16 Things Your Dog Doesn't Understand

☺ That he's not your superior

☺ The word 'No!'

☺ Anything else you tell him in plain English

☺ Why he shouldn't roll in the mud and then take a nap on your bed

☺ Why you all suddenly leave the room when he has a wind attack

☺ That you don't find it absolutely hilarious when, late one night, he suddenly starts staring at an empty corner of the room with teeth bared and hackles raised

☺ Precisely what's wrong with practising his fiercest, gruffest bark at three in the morning

☺ That it's not funny to carry your discarded underpants into the room with him in front of guests

- That the furniture is not there for his personal amusement
- Why it's wrong to back Auntie Joan into a corner and guard her
- Why your leg doesn't enjoy it as much as he does
- That other dogs' bottoms are not the most fascinating things in the world
- Why your cat has as much right to sit in the lounge as he has
- Why he should get into the bathtub if he doesn't want to
- Why he shouldn't steal the pâté off the table if he can reach it
- Why he shouldn't do exactly what he wants, basically

10 Amazing Books by Thomas Hardy About Fish

- The Bream of Casterbridge
- Tess of the Herring
- Far from the Madding Shoal
- Jude the Halibut
- The Mullet Major
- Desperate Tench
- Life's Little Minnows
- The Fins of Ethel Sardine
- Under the Grey-Green Sea
- The Return of the Salmon

... And 10 More by Charles Dickens

✕ A Tale of Two Trout

✕ Haddock and Son

✕ A Christmas Fish

✕ Oliver Tiddler

✕ Nicholas Coelacanth

✕ David Codderfield

✕ The Whitebait Papers

✕ The Old Curiosity Mackerel

✕ Little Coley

✕ Edwin Skate

11 Animals That Are Fat Bastards

☛ The pig

☛ The hippo

☛ The elephant

☛ The sea cow

☛ The brontosaurus

☛ The whale

☛ The sea lion

☛ The rhinoceros

☛ The toad

☛ The walrus

☛ The American bison

10 Rivals to the Teenage Mutant Ninja Turtles

◆ The Geriatric Radioactive Kung Fu Ocelots

◆ The Prepubescent Irradiated Jujitsu Wildebeest

◆ The Adolescent Disfigured Tai Chi Dormice

◆ The Menopausal Isotopic Karate Badgers
◆ The Retired Glowing Judo Wallabies
◆ The Middle-Aged Nuclear Origami Sheep
◆ The Thirty-Something Toxic Black Belt Guinea Pigs
◆ The Just-Toddling Freako Samurai Head Lice
◆ The Old-Before-Their-Time Half-Life Kamikaze Tree Shrews
◆ The Immature Plutonium Hitachi Bison

8 Different Kinds of Shrew You Couldn't Care Less About

☆ North African elephant shrew
☆ Giant elephant shrew
☆ Masked shrew
☆ Eurasian common shrew
☆ Eurasian water shrew
☆ Northern short-tailed shrew
☆ Bicoloured white-toothed shrew
☆ Sav's pygmy shrew (aka the Etruscan shrew)

11 Creatures Which Sound Rude

✶ The bustard
✶ The great tit
✶ The poodle
✶ The horny toad
✶ The cockatoo

✗ The pronghorn antelope
✗ The winkle
✗ The cockle
✗ The cock
✗ The ass
✗ The sperm whale

The Official Scientific Latin Names for Various Different Types of Dog Poo

☀ *Squigissimi* (Squidgies)
☀ *Moccari Admiratio* (Mocha Surprises)
☀ *Flavi Periculum* (Yellow Perils)
☀ *Rex Canii Fecii* (King Dog Plops)
☀ *Dimidium Liquorum Latere* (Semi-Liquid Lurkers)
☀ *Crispus Turbi* (Curly-Wurlies)
☀ *Clandestinus Imbuere Cumululi* (Stealthy Tan Clusters)
☀ *Fulvus Gigasere* (Brown Behemoths)
☀ *Odor Maximus* (Great Whiffies)
☀ *Cretosus Putrefacere* (Chalky Crumbles)

CULTURE SHOCK

6 Alternative Names for 'Man Friday' if Robinson Crusoe Had Found Him on a Different Day

- Man Monday
- Man Saturday
- Man Thursday
- Man Sunday
- Man Wednesday
- Man Tuesday

---

10 Stupid Ways to Try to Communicate the Philosophy of Socrates to the General Public

- ✗ An ice show spectacular
- ✗ A weekly sitcom
- ✗ Mime
- ✗ Semaphore
- ✗ As a series of complicated anagrams
- ✗ In skywriting
- ✗ Using The Smurfs or The Wombles

✗ Subliminally, during episodes of *T.J. Hooker*

✗ As a daily strip cartoon in the *Sun*

✗ Written on a small piece of paper hidden down your trousers

---

13 Stupid Things to Attempt to Take with You Into the National Gallery

☛ A flamethrower

☛ A large Gurkha knife

☛ An armoured vehicle

☛ A bag marked 'swag'

☛ A spray can and stencil

☛ A bucket of fresh dung and a catapult

☛ A frenzied Rottweiler

☛ A huge glass tank filled with ultra-destructive Death's-head moths

☛ Yourself, stark naked, except for a strap-on dildo attached to your forehead

☛ A party of epileptics, each carrying a brand new set of ginsu knives

☛ A large sheet of tracing paper and a stepladder

☛ A large container of industrial-strength paint stripper and a scraper

☛ A hammer and chisel in a bag marked 'Acme Statue Improvement Service'

10 Stupid Things to Attempt to Take Out of the National Gallery

◆ The piss
◆ One of the curators in a sack
◆ A wild animal (they haven't got any)
◆ The cloakroom
◆ The frame of the most valuable painting on display
◆ A girlie art student in a sack
◆ The foundations
◆ A cup of tea from the cafeteria, balanced on your head
◆ The floors
◆ *In the Park* by Claude Monet (it's in the Tate . . .)

10 Books Barbara Cartland Will Never Write

☆ *Gunfight at Apache Falls*
☆ *Nob Me, My Darling*
☆ *SS Panzer Death Unit*
☆ *Rogered are the Brave*
☆ *King Dong Meets the Lesbo Wife Swappers*
☆ *The Cisco Kid's Last Round-Up*
☆ *Confessions of a Proctologist*
☆ *Jism Merchants of Venus*
☆ *A Dialectic Approach to Practices of Semiotic Theory*
☆ *Royal Family Cannibal Holocaust*

11 Things Which Sound Better Than Marc Almond's Singing Voice

✗ Greasy chalk being slid extra slowly down a blackboard

✗ Someone cracking their knuckles right next to your ear

✗ A burp

✗ Bullfrogs calling for a mate across the bayou

✗ A dog farting

✗ Cats on the tiles

✗ The sound of your prized best china shattering into smithereens

✗ Hungry crows

✗ The worst karaoke performance you ever had the misfortune to sit through

✗ You in the bathtub

✗ Pretty much anything else

10 Stupid Things the Authors of This Book Have Done. (Honest!)

☺ Hit Ashley Kopitko in the face with a cream cake

☺ Stayed up all night looking for flying saucers

☺ Appeared on national television wearing women's tights, swimming trunks and towels

☺ Flicked V-signs at passengers out of a first-class railway carriage

☀ Bunked off school to eat choux buns and read DC comics

☀ *'Rhinoceros Men from Mars'* impressions along Bournemouth Promenade

☺ Held a children's birthday party in the middle of an A-level 'Government & Politics' class

☀ Made a home video for 'Born To Run', featuring a child's doll and a bottle of Domestos

☺ Driven to Southend on a whim, simply because it seemed like a good idea at the time

☀ Agreed that 4 January was a good publication date for their book *The Naughty 90s* – the one you've *really* never heard of ...

The Top 10 Television Shows in Belgium, 1990 (with Viewing Figures)

📺 *Ho, Ho, Grandma, You Know Some Good Tales* (4.2 million)

📺 *That's My Pet* (3.7 million)

📺 *Creosote Your Fence the Expert Way* (3.4 million)

📺 *My Good Auntie Gerta* (sitcom) (3.2 million)

📺 *A Short History of the Cheese* (2.95 million)

📺 *The Jolly Albert Monkey Show* (2.6 million)

- *How Our Parliament Does the Efficient Job We Expect of It* (2 million)
- *Knit Yourself a Sweater for Wintertime* (1.9 million)
- *Oh, How Domestic Life Can Have Its Funny Side Sometimes!* (1.7 million)
- *Oh, You Naughty Belgians!* (Reworking of *That's Life*) (1 million)

The Bottom 10 Television Shows in Belgium, 1990 (with Viewing Figures in Tens)

- ✕ *The Best of Belgian Variety* (1.7)
- ✕ *The Seven Wonders of Belgium* (1.4)
- ✕ *The Belgian Television Awards* 1990 (1.1)
- ✕ *What's On in Brussels* (0.8)
- ✕ *Your Local News* (0.7)
- ✕ *Matters Which Shaped Our Proud Nation* (0.6)
- ✕ *A Nation at War* (Belgium) (0.4)
- ✕ *Belgium's Rising New Comedy Stars of Tomorrow* (0.3)
- ✕ *Belgium 2000 – How We Will Be Living Tomorrow* (0.1)
- ✕ *Our Song for Europe 1990 – The Final Vote* (0.0)

The Top 10 Television Shows in Japan, 1990

- ☛ *Humiliate Your Friend or Workmate* (100 million)
- ☛ *Toko's Hilarious Dolphin Killing Challenge!* (97 million)

- ☛ *We Shall Rise Again!* (92 million)
- ☛ *Humiliate Your Spouse* (84 million)
- ☛ *Humiliate Your Children* (81 million)
- ☛ *Humiliate Your Honourable Parents* (79.5 million)
- ☛ *Humiliate Your Venerated Ancestors* (71.8 million)
- ☛ *Humiliate Total Strangers* (66 million)
- ☛ *Humiliate Yourself* (61 million)
- ☛ *Celebrity Seppuku (The Mishima Cup)* (57 million)

10 Storylines You'll Never See on *Coronation Street*

- ◆ Alf Roberts, under the influence of a possessed packet of fish fingers, hacks Ivy Tilsley to bits with a machete and hides her body in the deep freeze
- ◆ Deirdre Barlow has a torrid lesbian affair with Mavis Wilton
- ◆ Curly Watts blackmails Reg Holdsworth into leaving Betterbuys and in his new position decides to sell only fruit and vegetables with suggestive shapes
- ◆ The Rover's Return is demolished to make way for a new ring road – with Alec still inside
- ◆ Derek Wilton leaves his job to become chief product tester at a company manufacturing plastic love aids
- ◆ Mike Baldwin jacks in his job and sells all

his worldly goods to become a simple travelling troubadour

◆ Emily Bishop discovers she's three months pregnant, but who's the father? Chief suspects are Jack Duckworth and Kevin Webster

◆ Percy Sugden and Gail have a torrid affair, part of which includes acting out his strange fantasies involving jelly and runner beans

◆ Brian Tilsley comes back from the dead as a blood-crazed zombie who hideously disfigures Bet Lynch, although no one notices for five episodes

◆ Ken Barlow is suspended from school after allegations that he made all the boys in his class parade in front of him smothered in suntan oil, wearing only their football socks

10 of the Most Embarrassing Publications to Ask for in a Newsagent

☆ *Reliant Robin World*

☆ *Aircraft Spotter Monthly (incorporating The Virgin)*

☆ *Premature Ejaculation Sufferer*

☆ *Coprophilia Weekly*

☆ *Self-Abuse Gazette*

☆ *Game-Show Enthusiast*

☆ *The Vivisectionist*

☆ *UK Tasty Birds Contact Mag*

☆ *Pig Fancier*
☆ *Sunday Sport*

10 Things That Vincent van Gogh Couldn't Do

- Count up to two, using his ears
- Make full use of a Sony Walkman
- Keep more than one paintbrush behind his ears
- Wear a pair of sunglasses and keep them straight
- Wear a pair of matching stud earrings
- Impersonate someone with two ears
- Earn the nickname 'Dumbo'
- Put his hand on his heart and say that he never once mutilated his head
- Grin from ear to ear
- Tell if something was in stereo

10 Stupid Things That Leonardo da Vinci Could Have Been Doing in Order to Make the Mona Lisa Smile

- Opening and closing his flies in time to music
- Doing his impression of Michelangelo pissed
- Telling the one about Pope Julius II, the goat and the lasagne
- Demonstrating a prototype clockwork vibrator that he'd just invented

- ☀ Telling her that one day heavier-than-air flight would be possible
- ☀ A big wet juicy fart
- ☀ Saying that one day this painting would be hanging in the Louvre – which she misheard as 'loo'
- ☀ Painting, unaware that he had a big blob of green paint on his chin
- ☀ Tickling her nether regions with a long feather duster
- ☀ Telling her he was going to pay her ten times more than he actually was

---

9 Shakespeare Plays That Sound Like Titles of Soft-Porn Videos

Two Gentlemen of Verona

The Merry Wives of Windsor

Antony and Cleopatra

King John

As You Like It

Twelfth Night

Measure for Measure

The Taming of the Shrew

The Rape of Lucrece

---

1 Newspaper Named After Something with an Internal Temperature of 35,000,000°C

✗ The *Sun*

---

1 Newspaper Named After the Planet Venus

☞ The *Morning Star*

Bruce Springsteen and the E Street Band's Favourite Flavoured Crisps

◆ Bruce 'The Boss' Springsteen (lead vocals, guitar) – roast chicken

◆ 'Professor' Roy Bittan (piano, background vocals) – barbecue beef

◆ Clarence 'Big Man' Clemons (saxophone, background vocals) – tomato ketchup

◆ 'Phantom' Danny Federici (organ) – prawn cocktail

◆ Nils Lofgren (acoustic guitar, harmony vocals) – cheese 'n' onion

◆ Patti Scialfa (percussion, vocals) – smoky bacon

◆ Gary W. Tallent (bass, background vocals) – ready salted

◆ 'Mighty Max' Weinberg (drums, background vocals) – salt 'n' vinegar

13 Predictable TV Programmes You Always Get at Christmas

☆ The same boring old Disney cartoons, introduced by Rolf Harris

☆ *Von Ryan's Express* and/or *Help* and/or *Mary Poppins* and/or *The Great Escape* and *White Christmas*

☆ The *Morecambe and Wise Show* with Glenda Jackson in

☆ Some film by Steven Spielberg that you've already seen on video

☆ Some film by Steven Spielberg that's already been on TV

☆ The 22nd screening of *Carry On Up the Khyber* that was only marginally funny the first time you saw it

☆ Some has-been DJ visiting sick kids in hospital

☆ Something with Fred Astaire in (unfortunately, not his coffin)

☆ A celebrity edition of a popular game show that's actually more boring than the regular game show

☆ The Queen's Christmas message (yawn)

☆ Something hosted by Noel Edmonds, making you rush for the remote control

☆ Some dickheads singing carols

☆ *Chitty Chitty Bang Bang* (which is only entertaining because it sounds a bit like 'Shitty Shitty Bang Bang')

14 Stupid Films That Combine the Thrills of Gardening and War

☷ *A Greenhouse Too Far*

☷ *Apocalypse Patio*

☷ *Trellis Over the River Kwai*

☷ *The Blue Trug*

☷ *The Mulch of Iwo Jima*

☷ *The Heroes of the Garden Centre*

☷ *Hoe of Iron*

☷ *The Hosepipe Ban of Navarone*

☷ *Flora! Flora! Flora!*

☷ *Von Ryan's Shrub*

    The Longest Hardy Perennial
     633 Sprinkler
      F*O*R*K
     Sink the Dahlia

14 Stupid Specialist Subjects to Choose for *Mastermind*

- Owl-pummelling
- The history of dysentery, 1715–87
- The life and times of Maria Whittaker
- The life and times of Magnus Magnusson
- Badger whoopsies
- Previous *Mastermind* contestants
- Your own life and times
- Unpleasant things to do with twine
- Things you find in the plughole after a bath
- The light operettas of Karl Marx and Fredrick Engels
- Gordon of Khartoum's pubes
- The colour orange
- Things we don't know the answers to yet
- Questions to which *all* the answers are 'Austro-Hungary'

12 Unsuitable Performers to Entertain the Frail and Elderly

- Eric and his Pyrotechnics Par Excellence
- Mr Harwood & his Daredevil Stunt Kittens

- Leather Marion's Bondage Half-Hour
- The Sudden Loud Noise Experience
- DJ Ranking Leroy B's Sound System
- The Nudie Royal Lookalikes Show
- Sonja the Viper-Juggler and Bill
- The Nottingham Slamdancers (audience participation encouraged!)
- The Tyrolean Blindfolded Yodelling Tumblers
- Billy Jenkins's Horror Roadshow
- The Lash Brothers' Whipcrackaway Wild West Show
- Danny Tib's Dying Animal Impressions Show

The Number of Buttocks Possessed by 10 Prominent Poets

- ✕ John Dryden (2)
- ✕ Andrew Marvell (2)
- ✕ T.S. Eliot (2)
- ✕ John Donne (2)
- ✕ Ted Hughes (2)
- ✕ Stevie Smith (2)
- ✕ Arthur Clough (2)
- ✕ Alfred Lord Tennyson (2)
- ✕ Robert Frost (2)
- ✕ William Butler Yeats (2)

FAME AND FORTUNE

12 Nicknames the Elephant Man Had to Endure at School

- Floppy Skin
- Repugno
- Trunky
- Big Head
- Nellie
- Pachyderm Features
- Jumbo Bonce
- Deformo
- Snorky Jack
- Tusker
- Jumbo John
- Norman Lamont

13 Pop Stars with 12 Letters in Their Names

- Janet Jackson
- Chris de Burgh
- Kylie Minogue
- Cliff Richard
- Art Garfunkel
- Mark Knopfler
- Elvis Presley
- Jason Donovan
- Stevie Wonder
- Johnny Rotten
- Keith Richard
- Roger Daltrey
- New Kids On The

10 Stupid Things That Magnus Magnusson Will Never Say to Contestants on *Mastermind*

☆ Isn't this a crap university?
☆ You were absolutely useless on your specialist subject
☆ Not another boring civil servant
☆ Have you just farted?
☆ Weren't you once a man?
☆ I've run out of questions
☆ And at the buzzer, Mr Jenkins, I'm sorry to say you've scored fuck all
☆ You give your occupation as 'Goat Castrator'
☆ The first contestant tonight is dead ugly . . .
☆ Smartarse

5 Famous People Named After Fabrics

⚦ Billy Cotton
⚦ Robert Kilroy-Silk
⚦ Linda Lovelace
⚦ John Linen
⚦ Terry Lene

10 Stupid Things the Waltons Would Never Do

☀ Undermine capitalism
☀ Set fire to their homestead for the insurance money

- Indulge in mass incest
- Take part in a $60,000 armed bank robbery
- Tunnel under Walton's Mountain in search of valuable uranium deposits
- Join the Ku Klux Klan for a laugh
- Destroy state property in an orgy of wanton destruction
- Sell their children into bondage
- Wear goat masks and worship the devil in a big way
- Go to bed with the lights on

6 Greek Philosophers Who Were Also Rappers

- L.L. Cool Socrates
- Ice T. Plato
- M.C. Aristotle
- The Ranking Mr Pythagoras
- Grandmaster Diogenes and his Furious Five
- Run Pericles

17 Famous People Who Preferred to Be Known by Their Initials for Some Reason

- ✕ W.G. Grace
- ✕ H.G. Wells
- ✕ W.C. Fields
- ✕ A.A. Milne
- ✕ M.C. Hammer
- ✕ D.H. Lawrence
- ✕ e.e. cummings
- ✕ J.R.R. Tolkien
- ✕ T.S. Eliot
- ✕ P.D. James

✕ J.B. Priestley   ✕ W.H. Smith
✕ E.M. Forster   ✕ R. Dean Taylor
✕ W.H. Auden   ✕ A.J.P. Taylor
✕ L.L. Cool J

Famous People You Never Knew Slept Together

- ☛ Mao Tse Tung and Cleo Laine
- ☛ Pablo Picasso and Su Pollard
- ☛ Marilyn Monroe and Sir Alf Ramsey
- ☛ Norman Wisdom and Victoria Principal
- ☛ Rock Hudson and Liberace
- ☛ Queen Victoria, Gordon of Khartoum and Charles Darwin
- ☛ Pope John Paul and Diana Dors
- ☛ Florence Nightingale and The 4th Light Durham Infantry
- ☛ Albert Einstein and Gracie Fields
- ☛ Fatty Arbuckle and Rin Tin Tin
- ☛ Admiral Nelson and Joan Collins

17 Marx Brothers Who Never Made It . . .

(Everyone knows Groucho, Chico and Harpo; devoted fans will probably have heard of Zeppo and Gummo, who made rare appearances in Marx Brothers films – but hardly anyone knows about the other brothers who never made it into the movies . . .)

- ◆ Leppo   ◆ Homo
- ◆ Vommo   ◆ Flatulo

- Sucko
- Pricko
- Sypho
- Lino
- Incontinento
- Ringo
- Crossdressero
- Typhoido
- Nobbo
- Pervo
- Fellatio
- Thicko
- Sumo

10 Stupid Things That John F. Kennedy Might Have Said Just After He Was Shot

☆ Boy! Have I got a migraine!

☆ Ouch!

☆ I think I'm losing my mind

☆ Did you hear that?

☆ Say what?

☆ Oh shit!

☆ Whooo! Good shot!

☆ Anyone know a good brain surgeon?

☆ I need this like a hole in the head

☆ Now I'll never be able to give Teddy those driving lessons

The Great Philosophers' Favourite Biscuits

✗ Epicurus ('After tasting them, I would have to say Bourbons')

✗ Jeremy Bentham ('I usually have whatever everyone else is having')

✗ David Hume ('It is not actually ever possible to *truly know* which is your favourite biscuit')

- ☥ Jean-Jacques Rousseau ('Anything with no artificial preservatives and flavourings')

- ☥ Thomas Hobbes ('Chocolate Hob-Nobs! Do you want a fight about it?')

- ☥ René Descartes ('I like both Viscounts and Jammy Dodgers')

- ☥ Benedict de Spinoza ('I agree with Descartes about the Viscounts, but not about the Jammy Dodgers')

- ☥ Blaise Pascal ('I like whatever biscuit God thinks is nicest; that way, if He exists, He won't be offended at my choice of biscuit')

- ☥ Auguste Compte ('After taking a thoroughly scientific approach to the question, I have come to the conclusion that it is Ginger Nuts')

- ☥ Bertrand Russell ('I took the same approach, but for my money, it's Huntley & Palmer's Butter Biscuits')

- ☥ Jean-Paul Sartre ('To say one has a *favourite* biscuit is to admit the choice is purely subjective and that we cannot objectively know that one biscuit is any *better* than any other')

- ☥ Arthur Schopenhauer ('I don't care')

- ☥ Friedrich Nietzsche ('Garibaldis are the *Uberbiscuit* and tomorrow belongs to them!')

A List Stolen from Paul Hogan's Dustbin

☺ Platypus Arbroath

☺ Koala Glasgow

☺ Wallaby Selkirk
☺ Kanga Perth
☺ Funnel Web Spider Falkirk
☺ Possum Inverness
☺ Coral Snake East Kilbride
☺ Wombat Edinburgh
☺ Sheep O'Groats
☺ Emu Stoneybridge
☺ Crocodile Dundee ✓✓✓

14 Famous People with Rude Names

🔲 Urethra Franklin
🔲 Epididymis Bosch
🔲 Sir Arthur Colon Doyle
🔲 J. Arthur Wank
🔲 Mark Twat
🔲 Jackson Bollock
🔲 V.S. Nipple
🔲 Edgar Allen Poo
🔲 Charles Dickend
🔲 Jean-Paul Fartre
🔲 Lou Rawls (try saying it out loud)
🔲 William Shatner
🔲 e.e. cummings
🔲 Tony Hancock

The Real Names of Famous Movie Stars

✗ John Wayne (Marion Botty)
✗ Kirk Douglas (Ricky Dibble)

✗ Rudolph Valentino (Harry Sick)

✗ Humphrey Bogart (Dennis Snotrag)

✗ Orson Welles (Prince the Wonder Dog)

✗ Alan Ladd (Ernest Borgnine)

✗ Cary Grant (Archibald Leech)

✗ Ernest Borgnine (Alan Ladd)

✗ Cyd Charisse (Sid Charisse)

✗ Judy Garland (Frances Gumm)

✗ Alec Guinness (Alec Light-Ale)

✗ Marlon Brando (Marlon Stott)

✗ Zsa-Zsa Gabor (Doris Smedley)

✗ Norman Wisdom (Norman Stupid)

✗ Rod Steiger (Sheik Abdullah al Rahmani of Quatar)

✗ Burt Reynolds (Debbie Reynolds)

✗ Anthony Quinn (Pope Gregory XIV)

✗ Joseph Bottoms (Clint Sphincter)

✗ Ginger Rogers (Ginger Buggers)

ONCE UPON A TIME

8 Stupid Pieces of Furniture in King Arthur's Castle, in Addition to His Round Table

- Rectangular chair
- Square bookcase
- Octagonal sideboard
- Diamond-shaped cupboard
- Hexagonal bed
- Elliptical sofa
- Triangular bath
- Trapezoid wardrobe

The Christian Names of the 6 American Presidents Called 'James'

◆ James	◆ James
◆ James	◆ James
◆ James	◆ James

The Christian Name of the 1 American President Called 'Zachary'

☆ Zachary

15 Reasons to Be Glad You Weren't Alive in the 14th Century

☥ It was utter crap back then

☥ The Church would burn you alive for having a wart or saying 'Here, kitty, kitty' or being caught in possession of a broom

☥ The only cure for toothache was to smash your head repeatedly against a wall until it hurt worse than your tooth

☥ You usually died before you were old enough to vote

☥ But then, you didn't have the vote anyway

☥ People with bubonic plague were everywhere, and they put you off your dinner

☥ You had to dance round a fucking maypole every May

☥ You spent from dawn until dusk up to your knees in shit

☥ There was no *Playboy* or *Custom Car* magazine. You had to read the Bible

☥ But then, you probably couldn't read anyway

☥ Lepers would come along and breathe on you

☥ All your orifices officially belonged to the lord of the manor

- ✗ By law, you had to practise archery, which is dead boring and hurts the fingers
- ✗ Your only entertainment would be watching a field lie fallow
- ✗ You wouldn't be alive now to see Julia Roberts

10 Things Viking Berserkers Were Renowned For

- ☺ Going berserk
- ☺ Cutting people's heads off
- ☺ Going purple in the face
- ☺ Screaming a lot
- ☺ Spinning in circles with a two-handed battle axe
- ☺ Thrashing about
- ☺ Foaming at the mouth
- ☺ Glazed expressions
- ☺ Dribbling profusely during combat
- ☺ Finishing fighting two hours after everybody else

10 Things Viking Berserkers Were Not Renowned For

- Baking good cakes
- Well-reasoned debate
- Charm
- Poise
- Elegance
- Cunning battle plans

- Good dress sense
- Having a lot upstairs
- An active sense of irony
- Washing behind their ears

10 Stupid Reasons to Be Glad You Weren't Alive in Victorian England

- ✕ Queen Victoria was even uglier than our queen
- ✕ All the women were frigid, and all the men were perverts
- ✕ You had to wear stupid pompous clothes and be polite all the time
- ✕ Jack the Ripper might get you
- ✕ Your employer had the legal right to strap your bare bottom
- ✕ Everyone thought steam engines were a bloody big deal
- ✕ If you think you're poor now, you'd be poorer then
- ✕ *All* the political parties were conservative
- ✕ Noblemen could force your children to go up their chimneys
- ✕ The middle classes were even more pompous and insufferable than they are today

8 Stupid Reasons Why the Romans Built Straight Roads

- ☛ To stop the Assyrians opening up corner shops

☞ The bend had yet to be invented

☞ Romans had no sense of direction and needed all the help they could get

☞ They were worried that Celts would smear slippery woad on the corners

☞ Chariots were not equipped with steering wheels

☞ They were scared of druids lurking in dark corners

☞ If they'd had bends, a legion might not see another legion coming the opposite way and collide head on

☞ Romans were notoriously prone to travel sickness

Nicknames of British Prime Ministers 1855–1924

◆ Viscount Palmerston ('Baldy')

◆ Earl Russell ('Dusty')

◆ The Earl of Derby ('Skipper')

◆ William Ewart Gladstone ('Basher')

◆ Benjamin Disraeli, Earl of Beaconsfield ('Spud')

◆ The Marquis of Salisbury ('Fatty')

◆ The Earl of Rosebery ('Stinker')

◆ Arthur James Balfour ('Nobby')

◆ Sir Henry Campbell-Bannerman ('Pee-Wee')

◆ Herbert Henry Asquith ('Bazza')

◆ David Lloyd George ('That Welsh Git')

◆ Andrew Bonar Law ('Randy Andy')
◆ Stanley Baldwin ('Guffer')
◆ James Ramsay MacDonald ('Bo-Bo')

10 Things Which Pharaoh Rameses III Would Not Be Able to Comprehend

☆ Heavier-than-air flight
☆ Escalators
☆ Julian Clary
☆ The music of Henry Mancini
☆ A microwave pizza
☆ *GQ* magazine
☆ A CD player
☆ Picasso
☆ Germ warfare
☆ Why anyone buys a Skoda

10 Unlikely Vikings

𝘹 Wulf the Sensible
𝘹 Olaf the Interior Decorator
𝘹 Frank the Berserker
𝘹 Ethelred Bottom Scratcher
𝘹 Sedring the Mediocre
𝘹 Bjorn of Arabia
𝘹 Horsa the Rather Nice
𝘹 Tubørg the Ticklish
𝘹 Kraken the Chubby
𝘹 Wülfberg the Fresh-Smelling

THE AMAZING WORLD OF CONFECTIONERY

13 Stupid Sweets of the 1970s That You Wish You Could Still Buy

- ☺ Spangles
- ☺ Treets
- ☺ Mint Cracknel
- ☺ Ice Breaker
- ☺ Aztec
- ☺ Supermousse
- ☺ Bazooka Joe
- ☺ Rupert Bar
- ☺ Golden Nugget chewing gum

☀ Spanish Gold sweet tobacco
☀ Pink Panther Bar
☀ Space Dust
☀ Cresta (OK, so it's a drink)

14 Stupid Names for Sweets That Don't Exist, But if They Did, You'd be Very Embarrassed Asking for Them

🛍 Wobbly Bobblies
🛍 Chocolate Bottoms
🛍 Zitties
🛍 Williemints
🛍 Knickie Knackie Knooes
🛍 Big Ones
🛍 Noblet Crunch
🛍 Whizzleybums
🛍 Spunky Pieces
🛍 Raspberry Nob-ends
🛍 Crunchy Bumwipes
🛍 Fatty-Fatty Gobble Bars
🛍 Nutty Pus Creams
🛍 Candy Verrucas

9 Stupid Things to Do with a Bar of Chocolate

✗ Throw it in the bin
✗ Unwrap it, smear it with axle grease and then give it to a loved one
✗ Use it as a smear-on deodorant

- ✘ Eat half, then offer to sell it back to the sweet shop for half the price you bought it for
- ✘ Smear it all over your face and pretend to be 18 months old
- ✘ Melt it down and use it as yummy eyeshadow
- ✘ Jump up and down on it, to make your feet look dirtier than they really are
- ✘ Give the dog a bite before you have one
- ✘ Attempt to smoke it

10 Stupid Sets of Bubble Gum Cards You Wouldn't Bother to Collect

- ☛ Soccer Stars' Brothers
- ☛ Eminent Belgian Ear, Nose and Throat Specialists
- ☛ Colours of the Rainbow
- ☛ Shoes of the Kings and Queens of England
- ☛ TV-AM Presenters
- ☛ Complex Equations & Formulae
- ☛ Soccer Stars with Their Backs Turned to the Camera
- ☛ Stars of Shinty
- ☛ Greek Philosophers (turn them over to form a giant 18″ x 12″ picture of Diogenes!)
- ☛ Famous People with Nosebleeds

HOME, SWEET HOME

10 Stupid Things to Be Left in a Will

◆ Custody of a pet warthog called Trevor

◆ Custody of a pet warthog called anything else

◆ Enormous debts

◆ A wheel from a 1984 Lada Riva 1200

◆ A map to find hidden treasure, with the X missing

◆ Two Toffets and a Mint Imperial

◆ A postcard from Malaga with the stamp torn off

◆ The solicitor's bill

◆ The deceased's treasured collection of Des O'Connor records

◆ The body

10 Stupid Addresses That You Wouldn't Want to Have

☆ Cheapo Avenue

☆ Condemned Crescent

☆ Syphilis Grove

☆ Wrong Side of Town Drive

☆ Very High Crime Rate Street

☆ Cesspit Place

☆ Site for the Forthcoming Ring Road Lane

☆ Unbelievably High Community Charge Terrace

☆ Cardboard City

☆ Death Row

10 Things You Wouldn't Want to Hear from Your Grandmother

☥ Her death rattle

☥ 'Slip me your tongue, big boy!'

☥ 'Ta-daa! How's this for the body of an eighty-year-old woman?'

☥ 'When I was twenty, Adolf and I were so in love, but he left me when your father was born . . .'

☥ 'And I'm leaving every single penny of my £600,000 estate to Tiddles even though I only bought him this afternoon'

☥ 'As you're my favourite grandchild I decided to have your name tattooed just inside my thigh. Look . . .'

☥ 'And here's the nice lime green sleeveless

pullover with matching mittens and balaclava I've knitted for your birthday'

☧ 'Have you ever wondered what it feels like to have each of your fingers pulled out of their sockets one at a time by a berserk old age pensioner?'

☧ 'Guess what! James Last is in town and I've got a spare ticket for his 24-hour Big Band-a-thon!'

☧ 'Cooooeeeee! It's time for you to change my surgical stockings. I hope my boil hasn't burst again!'

10 Things You Wouldn't Want to Receive in the Post

☀ Any note made up from letters cut out of old newspapers

☀ Anything from a solicitor

☀ Your loved one's head, giftwrapped

☀ A reply to your lonely hearts ad, beginning 'I'm out on parole . . .'

☀ An unbelievably difficult to understand mailing from *Reader's Digest* or *Which?* promising discounted subscriptions, the chance to win £500,000 and a free gift (which invariably turns out to be an HB pencil)

☀ Anything that smells of plastic explosive

☀ A letter that starts 'Following the reintroduction of National Service . . .

☀ A letter from your partner's secret lover, that you open by mistake

☀ A letter from your parents saying that you were, in fact, adopted

☀ Photographs of you and a domestic pet caught in a *very* compromising position, with an anonymous note demanding £30,000 – or the negatives will be sent to the press, the RSPCA and Robinson's Jam

12 Things That Toddlers Have an Uncanny Ability to Do

▫ Wake up from a deep, deep sleep just 90 seconds after you finally get to bed

▫ Cry for one minute longer than you can possibly tolerate

▫ Poo themselves in a big way, 30 seconds after you've struggled to change their nappy

▫ Forget to walk, speak or generally act cute as soon as your friends or relatives are watching

▫ Scream their lungs out as soon as your car gets caught in a stationary motorway traffic jam

▫ Lose all appetite as soon as you've finished slaving over their favourite dinner

▫ Hide your keys in a completely different (and equally inaccessible) place each time

▫ Spurn expensive and impressive toys in favour of a cornflake packet and two yoghurt pots

- Find the only Biro without a cap when your back's turned for 8 seconds
- Always manage to find one of your eyes when playing with a blunt instrument
- Throw up only on clothes that have to be dry cleaned
- Develop mysterious bruises and other marks on their skin 10 minutes before the health visitor comes

20 Stupid Things Your Parents Say to You When You're Young

- ✗ Don't do that, you'll go blind
- ✗ Stop picking it, you'll get a hole there
- ✗ It'll put hairs on your chest
- ✗ I'll tell you when you're older
- ✗ Ask your mother
- ✗ Let the air get to it
- ✗ Don't leave it, there are starving children in Africa
- ✗ You treat this house like a hotel
- ✗ Have you done your homework?
- ✗ Wait till your father gets home
- ✗ Don't spend it all at once
- ✗ Don't rock the chair – you'll loosen the joints
- ✗ Don't read at the table
- ✗ Don't play with your food
- ✗ . . . Because I say so
- ✗ You wait until I get you home

- ✕ Santa won't come if you're not asleep
- ✕ Have you cleaned your teeth?
- ✕ Have you cleaned your hands?
- ✕ Don't say that, dear, it's not nice

18 Stupid Things You're Scared of When You're a Kid

- ☞ Being separated from your mummy and daddy in a huge department store
- ☞ Brussels sprouts
- ☞ Your winkie disappearing down the plughole when the bath water runs out
- ☞ Parents' evening at school
- ☞ The bogieman under the bed
- ☞ The bogieman under the stairs
- ☞ The bogieman in the shed
- ☞ Bigger kids
- ☞ The Daleks
- ☞ Being sent to boarding school
- ☞ The dark
- ☞ Your mummy telling your daddy, when he comes home from work, that you were very naughty
- ☞ What your daddy will do after your mummy has told him that you were very naughty
- ☞ The monsters in *Carry On Screaming*
- ☞ The rubber dinosaurs in *10,000,000 Years BC*

- ☛ Mummy throwing all your comics away
- ☛ The school medical and the peculiar 'coughing' test
- ☛ Big dogs jumping up at you

8 Stupid Suggestions for Summer Outings for the Kids

- ◆ Take them to Battersea to watch the doggies being put to sleep
- ◆ A day trip to Milton Keynes
- ◆ Drive endlessly round and round the M25 (keep the windows wound up tight, swerve around a lot, chain smoke and turn the heating full on until the kids feel sick and want to go home and lie down)
- ◆ A Halal meat slaughterhouse – to find out how other people live
- ◆ The doctor's surgery (to have totally superfluous and incredibly painful vaccination against green monkey rot or ostrich distemper)
- ◆ The Shed End at Chelsea
- ◆ Southend on a bank holiday (pretty much the same thing)
- ◆ A local Labour Party constituency meeting (also very similar)

11 Stupid Things Children Always Bring Home from School with Them

- ☆ Crappy balsa wood models that you have to go into raptures about
- ☆ Infections

- ☆ Crazes for nasty, overpriced plastic Japanese toys
- ☆ The F-word
- ☆ Their lunch boxes, minus the lid
- ☆ Strange ideas about human reproduction
- ☆ Invitations to parents' evenings – three months too late
- ☆ Requests for copious amounts of cash
- ☆ Scabby, blood-encrusted knees which they want you to kiss better . . .
- ☆ Friends who pick their nose and then cry until they're taken home
- ☆ Somebody else's gym kit

10 Things You Wouldn't Want to Find on Your Doorstep at Midnight

- Your ex-girlfriend, cradling an infant in her arms
- A circus clown carrying a carving knife
- Two tons of fresh pig manure
- A naked Maori with a glazed expression
- Four nuns spending a penny and giggling to themselves
- A midget with a cutthroat razor
- Two midgets with two cutthroat razors
- The pilots of the missing Flight 19, each carrying a bouquet of fresh roses
- A long-dead relative
- A wreath with your name on it

10 Stupid Things to Run up Behind Your Grandad and Yell

- ☀ BOO!
- ☀ Die, pig-dog *Englischer* soldier!
- ☀ Give us all yer cash, old man!
- ☀ Grandad! Quick! Your buttocks are on fire!
- ☀ Rhinoceros! Rhinoceros!
- ☀ Stuka attack! Down, boys! Down!
- ☀ Grandad! It's the hospital on the phone . . . they want your pacemaker back . . .
- ☀ Grandad! Grandad! Your catheter's leaking!
- ☀ They've found out! Run for it!
- ☀ Granny's dead!

12 Stupid Things to Take Into the Bath With You

- ▪ A plugged-in four-bar electric heater
- ▪ A school of barracuda
- ▪ A surfboard
- ▪ Quick-setting cement
- ▪ 40lb of instant potato mix and a whisk
- ▪ A speedboat
- ▪ Four boy scouts and a Polaroid camera
- ▪ Cat wee-wee scented foam bath lotion
- ▪ A dead wildebeest
- ▪ Your water wings

    🎮 A deep-sea diver's outfit
    🎮 Your clothes

11 Stupid Things to Buy for a Blind Relative

✗ A ticket to a *Son et Lumière* show
✗ A jigsaw puzzle
✗ A Charlie Chaplin video
✗ A ticket to see Marcel Marceau in performance
✗ A pair of binoculars
✗ A car
✗ A shaving mirror
✗ A porno mag
✗ A white stick with a castor stuck on the end
✗ A stick which they *think* is white . . .
✗ A Nintendo Gameboy

10 Things You Don't Want to Live Next Door To

☞ Sellafield
☞ The world's only outdoor urine storage vat
☞ Millwall football club
☞ A free-range cobra farm
☞ The place where the army tests the calibration on its new howitzers
☞ A halfway house for burglars and arsonists trying to go straight

☛ Mount Etna
☛ A graveyard full of tormented souls
☛ Britain's largest pig farm
☛ An experimental Semtex factory

21 Things Your Children Will Always Ask You

◆ Where did I come from?
◆ Can I have my pocket money in advance?
◆ Can I stay up and watch the horror film?
◆ Can I have some money?
◆ Can I have a tasty jacket like Leon's?
◆ Can I have some more money?
◆ Will you do my homework for me?
◆ Can I have some more money?
◆ Why haven't you washed my gym kit?
◆ Can I have some more money?
◆ Can my friend come round to play?
◆ Can I have some more money?
◆ Can I have trainers like on the telly?
◆ Can I have some more money?
◆ Do I have to have a bath?
◆ Can I have some more money?
◆ Why can't I have some more money?
◆ Can I have the most expensive toy you've ever heard of for Christmas?
◆ Can I have some more money?
◆ Why can't I stay out till 3 a.m.?
◆ Have you got any money?

12 Things You Wouldn't Want to See in Your Front Garden

☆ 3 dogs shagging

☆ A crashed UFO

☆ A squat established by 11 itinerant Hell's Angels

☆ The corpse of your dead hamster Joey, risen from the grave

☆ A sign saying 'Compulsorily Purchased'

☆ Someone who's just escaped from an asylum, smiling and brandishing a meat cleaver

☆ NATO exercises

☆ An unexploded WWII doodlebug, ticking

☆ A huge heap of glowing toxic waste

☆ A slowly widening chasm

☆ Most of your roof

☆ Your wife dancing stark naked, yelling 'Yoo hoo! Neighbours! Look at me!'

12 Stupid Things to Say When Your Child Asks 'What Did You Do in the War, Daddy?'

- I was a traitor who spied for the enemy
- Napalmed an entire village. It was bloody brilliant
- Tortured anyone I could get my hands on
- Shat myself
- Shot myself
- Hid under a bed in Canada

- ☥ Peeled 600,000 lbs of potatoes
- ☥ Went AWOL for two years
- ☥ Dressed as a woman to avoid conscription
- ☥ Killed 317 of my own men by accident
- ☥ Killed 317 of my own men on purpose
- ☥ Fought for Hitler

11 Stupid Things Children Say When They're in the Back of Your Car

- ☀ I want to go home
- ☀ I don't want to go home
- ☀ Are we nearly there yet?
- ☀ I want to be sick
- ☀ I want to go wee-wee
- ☀ I've just been sick
- ☀ I've just done a wee-wee
- ☀ Can I sit in the front?
- ☀ I'm hungry
- ☀ I'm thirsty
- ☀ Wheeeeee! Big Jobs!

14 Stupid Comments That Your Grandfather Always Comes out with

- ☻ Call this art? My four-year-old granddaughter could do better
- ☻ Don't call them animals! Animals don't behave like that
- ☻ And you could still get change from a shilling
- ☻ People have no respect these days

- Whatever happened to tunes you could whistle?
- They don't even look like motor cars nowadays
- In my day that was a month's wages
- Shoot the lot of 'em!
- They don't build them like they used to
- I didn't fight in the war so you could have a haircut like that!
- Here's two bob. Don't spend it all at once, lad
- Kids today don't know when they're well off
- All you get on TV these days is sex and violence
- I remember when . . . (blah, blah, blah, blah)

10 Stupid Things to Attempt with a Flymo
✗ Conversation

✗ A Mike Tyson haircut

✗ Ritual circumcision

✗ Solving the problems of the Middle East

✗ Pubic topiary

✗ A game of chess

✗ Manned flight

✗ Thought transference

✗ Sexual relations

✗ The forging of a brave new world

12 Things Sir Ranulph Fiennes Would Almost Certainly Discover If He Led an Expedition Down the Back of Your Sofa

- ☞ Stale salted peanuts
- ☞ Several cwt of fluff
- ☞ A leaky Biro
- ☞ A Cadbury's Creme Egg wrapper
- ☞ A two-pence piece
- ☞ The contraceptive pill you thought you took yesterday
- ☞ A sock
- ☞ A crumpled-up Heineken can from the last party you had
- ☞ The lost remote control for the TV set
- ☞ The dog's chew bone
- ☞ Your missing house keys
- ☞ Something sticky

11 Things Sir Ranulph Fiennes Would Be Most Unlikely to Discover If He Led an Expedition Down the Back of Your Sofa

- ◆ Fresh salted peanuts
- ◆ Anything you'd want to eat
- ◆ The lost hoard of Bluebeard
- ◆ The secret of the Universe
- ◆ A cure for Parkinson's disease
- ◆ El Dorado
- ◆ A short cut to the West Indies

- ◆ Peckham
- ◆ A clean patch
- ◆ A £20 note
- ◆ Lord Lucan

14 Surnames You Don't Want to Be Born With

- ☆ Pratt
- ☆ Boggs
- ☆ Widdlecombe
- ☆ Bottoms
- ☆ Crapper
- ☆ Wanklin
- ☆ Cox
- ☆ Shatz
- ☆ Stroker
- ☆ Spunkmeyer
- ☆ Gay
- ☆ Fish
- ☆ Tweazlegrunter
- ☆ Hitler

12 Convenient Excuses for Not Giving Your Child Any Pocket Money

- I'm saving up so we can go to Disneyland
- You're adopted, so we don't have to give you anything
- It's the Tories . . . (Even five-year-olds know they're to blame for *everything* . . .)
- I daren't: God took Granny when she asked for too much pocket money
- Mummy and I don't love you enough . . .
- You'll understand when you're older
- Your daddy drinks all our money, so blame him . . .
- They've stopped making half-pence pieces, darling

- Who cares what you want?
- Only boys get pocket money . . .
- Only girls get pocket money . . .
- I said the boy next door could have your pocket money, because he asked so nicely . . .

---

10 Things It Would be Stupid to Say to Someone Who's Thinking of Buying Your House

- Excuse the mess: the parapsychologists have only just left . . .
- How we laughed when we heard that Dennis Nilsen was the previous owner!
- I hear the mortgage rate's going up by another 12% soon . . .
- I'll take a tenner for it
- Rats? No, it's too damp for rats
- After the fifth break-in, we decided that enough was enough . . .
- That? Oh, we think that's a bloodstain
- The Hell's Angels next door are really very friendly
- Piss off
- Try not to lean against that wall if you can help it . . .

10 Stupid and Heartless Things to Put in Your Child's Stocking at Christmas

- Nothing
- Last year's presents
- Last year's presents, all smashed up
- A rusty mantrap
- The child, head first
- The family cat on a skewer
- The contents of your wheelie bin
- The contents of your bowels
- Yourself, disguised as the rampaging, throat-slitting, totally evil bogieman ...
- A note of abuse from Santa

11 Things Babies Excel At

- ✕ Crying at 15-second intervals around the clock
- ✕ Pooing at 15-second intervals around the clock
- ✕ Soaking up your cash like a sponge
- ✕ Giving vile relatives an excuse to 'pop over' every other day and eat all your chocolate digestives
- ✕ Soaking up even more money
- ✕ Spewing up on something that has to be expensively dry cleaned
- ✕ Spewing up on something that can't be cleaned at all
- ✕ Finding something vile – and putting it straight in their mouths

✕ Giving complete strangers an excuse to come over and bother you in Tesco's

✕ Giving parents an excuse to bore everyone to death with accounts of their every fart, puke, whiff or dribble

✕ Forcing you to sell your beloved MG Midget to get a 'sensible' four-door family saloon

16 Stupid Things to Say When Visiting a Sick Relative

☛ So, how long have you got then?

☛ Need any help with the rectal thermometer?

☛ Breathe on me! Breathe on me!

☛ God, you look like shit!

☛ Can I have first dibs on your jewellery?

☛ Old Mrs Higgins had that. She died

☛ Good morning, I'm the Grim Reaper . . .

☛ You smell, I'm going to have to leave now

☛ I thought only sheep caught that . . .

☛ Fire! Fire! Everybody out! Quickly!

☛ The will's in the cupboard, is it?

☛ You look forty years older! I didn't recognise you . . .

☛ Chemists get prescriptions mixed up all the time, you know

☛ It *starts* as a cold, yes . . .

☛ You're hallucinating: I'm not really here

☛ So, just two weeks, eh? What, oh, they hadn't told you . . .

8 Stupid Things to Put on Your Answerphone

◆ 'I'm here, but I can't be bothered to answer you'

◆ 'I'm not remotely interested in what you have to say, so don't bother leaving a message'

◆ A message pretending to be someone else

◆ 'Thanks for dialling Leather Fantasy Line. Please leave your name, address and fantasy after the tone . . .'

◆ A message in Dutch

◆ 'You have dialled the wrong number. Please try again . . .'

◆ The Nepalese national anthem

◆ A four-ton weight

10 Stupid Things to Buy for a Deaf Relative

☆ A copy of *What Hi-Fi?* magazine

☆ A large ornamental ear trumpet

☆ A talking parrot

☆ The new Sting album

☆ A cordless phone

☆ A chiming doorbell

☆ A tape of Frederick Forsyth reading *The Day of the Jackal*

☆ A guide dog

☆ A radio alarm clock

☆ A balloon to fix to their bottom so they can tell if they fart

10 Things Your Children Always Tell You When It's Too Late

✗ Mum, it's cookery today. I've got to bring in a pound of flour, four ounces of raisins, two eggs and a bottle of vanilla essence . . .

✗ Mum, I'm in the school play this afternoon. I'm a Hebrew onlooker. Can you make me a costume please?

✗ Mum, it's cross-country today. Have you washed my kit?

✗ Mum, it's harvest festival in assembly today and I need lots of tins and biscuits and bread and jam and cereals to give to the old people

✗ Mum, it's open evening tonight. Do you want to come?

✗ Mum, I've put my name down for the school trip to Russia. Can I have £150 for the deposit today, please?

✗ Mum, it's swimming today and I've lost my trunks . . .

✗ Mum, Mrs Jones is leaving today and I have to give her a card and a present . . .

✗ Mum, it's crafts today and I need a ball of green wool, a ball of red wool and two No. 5 needles . . .

✗ Mum, it's Show and Tell today and I've got to bring in a book on Oliver Cromwell . . .

MIND AND BODY

12 Stupid (But Polite) Ways to Describe Someone Who's Absolutely Obese

- Plump
- Happy
- Jolly
- Big boned
- Chubby
- Stout
- Quite big
- Friendly
- Cuddly
- Well built
- A healthy appetite
- A nice personality

10 Stupid Complaints to Go to Your Doctor with

- My car engine misfires at about 45 m.p.h. in top gear
- My neighbours are always holding noisy parties
- This Elton John record I bought yesterday is warped
- Two of the oranges I got from the greengrocer are mouldy
- A bit of my filling has chipped off

- One of the entries on my Visa statement is wrong
- There's a man at work who's always making lewd suggestions and brushing up against me by the filing cabinet
- That new Arnold Schwarzenegger film is awful
- My guttering needs replacing
- It rained the whole time we were there

The 11 Most Embarrassing Times to Pass Wind

- ✗ During the one minute silence at the Remembrance Day ceremony
- ✗ Live, on *Wogan*
- ✗ While proposing
- ✗ While delivering a stern lecture on the evils of flatulence in public
- ✗ While being knighted by the Queen for services rendered in protecting the environment
- ✗ During a display of synchronised underwater swimming
- ✗ While sitting on your partner's face
- ✗ While having an internal examination carried out by two burly customs officers
- ✗ During the finals of the World Let's See Who Can Eat 19 Boiled Eggs Without Farting contest
- ✗ During the middle of your delicate haemorrhoid operation
- ✗ When you say 'I do'

9 Parts of the Body That You Could Quite Easily Do Without

☛ Earlobe

☛ The dangly thing at the back of your throat

☛ Appendix

☛ Little toe

☛ Belly button

☛ Tonsils

☛ Armpit hair

☛ That big spot on your bottom

☛ Nipples (if you're a man)

10 Things Blondes Have – Apart from More Fun

◆ Blonde hair

◆ Dark roots

◆ Dandruff that's harder to spot

◆ More chance of getting seriously sunburned

◆ More chance than average of winning a Darryl Hannah lookalike contest

◆ Very little chance of winning a Diana Ross lookalike contest

◆ A good chance of marrying Rod Stewart (for what that's worth)

◆ Lots of men automatically assuming they're stupid

- Lots of women automatically assuming they're stupid
- Lots of tired old clichés used about them – like 'blondes have more fun'

---

10 Sure Signs That You're Stark Raving Mad

- ☆ Mags from Aha appears by your bedside every night and whispers to you about the cheeses of the world
- ☆ You walk into the office one day, stark naked except for a British Home Stores bag over your head
- ☆ You proposed to Derbyshire
- ☆ You *know* you're being followed everywhere by a branch of Debenhams
- ☆ You think the government cares about you
- ☆ Your sex life revolves around chives and an Argos catalogue
- ☆ You keep bombarding the BBC with letters to bring back *Doctor Who*
- ☆ You dial 0898 numbers
- ☆ There's a C5 in your driveway
- ☆ Your marriage certificate says you're married to a Lady Diana Spencer

---

10 Things You Wouldn't Want to Sit Down on by Accident

- The cat
- A rusty 4-inch spike
- Your dinner
- Your last packet of cigarettes

   ✗ A red-hot poker
   ✗ A red ants' nest
✗ Your collection of exotic bird eggs
  ✗ What the cat's just retched up
  ✗ A complete stranger's hand
  ✗ A large predatory animal

12 People Not to Have Your Nose Job Modelled on

☺ Sir Ralph Halpern
☺ Barbra Streisand
☺ Barbra Streisand's dad
☺ General de Gaulle
☺ Karl Malden
☺ W.C. Fields
☺ Henry Cooper
☺ Pinocchio
☺ Bob Hope
☺ Cyrano de Bergerac
☺ Jimmy Durante
☺ General Urko, from *Planet of the Apes*

10 Quite Appealing Ways to Die

▪ Orgasmed to death by Charlie's Angels
▪ Overdosing on calories after eating 20 servings of chocolate fudge cake and ice cream
▪ Submerged beneath a tidal wave of Glenlivet and ice
– That's about it, really

15 of the Most Embarrassing Things to ask for in a Chemist

✗ Their biggest bottle of super strength acne lotion

✗ Intimate wipes

✗ Pile ointment

✗ Breath freshener

✗ Diarrhoea medicine

✗ Panty shields

✗ Sore nipple cream

✗ Bikini-line strip wax

✗ 'Super Plus' tampons

✗ Nasal hair trimmers

✗ Douche solution

✗ Flavoured condoms

✗ 'Extra Small' condoms

✗ Anything at all to do with warts

✗ Anything at all to do with male virility problems

12 Stupid Things to Ask a Plastic Surgeon for

☛ A nose seven times as large

☛ A 30 AA bust

☛ Bags under your eyes

☛ The bits he removed from Michael Jackson, in a box

☛ Liposuction of the testicles

☛ A hunchback

☛ A harelip

☛ A face drop

☛ A club foot

☛ Ears like Prince Charles

☛ All the features of a pencil-necked geek

☛ A huge bill

The 10 Most Common Objects Removed from Bodily Orifices on Friday Nights in the Casualty Ward

◆ Marrows smeared with taramasalata

◆ Torches with rubber handles

◆ Souvenir models of the Eiffel Tower

◆ Cans of shaving foam (half empty)

◆ Umbrellas (half opened)

◆ Policemen's truncheons

◆ Large Toblerones

◆ Rolled up copies of *TV Quick* (that's the way, uh huh, uh huh . . .)

◆ Gerbils

◆ Hands (still attached to their rather embarrassed owners)

The 7 Physiological Wonders of the Modern World

☆ Prince Charles's ears

☆ Chesney Hawkes's growth

☆ Sir Ralph Halpern's nose

☆ Jeremy Beadle's smile

☆ Jim Davidson's brain
☆ Roy Hattersley's saliva glands
☆ Bruce Forsyth's wig

10 Things That are Bad for You

✠ Anything you enjoy
✠ A bucket of Polish vodka
✠ Throwing yourself into a live volcano
✠ Wayward women
✠ Married men
✠ Radioactive bath towels
✠ Running into a germ warfare plant and inhaling sharply
✠ Consuming 800 cheeseburgers in 30 minutes
✠ The working week
✠ Death

10 Things That Look Like Bogies

☀ Swarfega
☀ Sultanas
☀ Squashed peas
☀ Rolled-up bits of dried glue
☀ Other bogies
☀ Tiny bits of Blu-tack
☀ Dried egg on your shirt cuff
☀ Capers
☀ Sandwich spread
☀ A giant amoeba

10 People You're Unlikely Ever to See Naked

- Pope John Paul
- Neil Kinnock
- Arthur Scargill
- George Bush
- Mrs Bush
- P.D. James
- David Mellor
- Claire Rayner
- Your Sunday School teacher
- Ted Hughes

14 Stupid Places to Relieve Yourself

✗ In your living room

✗ In the winner's enclosure at Ascot

✗ In a crowded lift

✗ Directly on to exposed power cables

✗ Over the boss's car

✗ At the top of the Eiffel Tower

✗ Live on national television

✗ On the desk at your job interview

✗ In the confessional

✗ In the font at a christening

✗ Over the puppy, in an act of revenge . . .

✗ In the supermarket's dairy produce cabinet

✗ In the fast lane of the M25

✗ Up the leg of the beefiest skinhead you can find

12 Stupid Examples of Body Language Guaranteed Not to Attract Anyone of the Opposite Sex

- ☛ Picking your nose but trying to make it look like you're scratching it
- ☛ Picking your nose but trying to make it look like you're squeezing a blackhead
- ☛ Getting that annoying bit of earwax out of your ear with a Biro
- ☛ Scratching your crotch frantically
- ☛ Nodding constantly and smiling inanely
- ☛ Trying to touch your left ear with your right hand, over the top of your head
- ☛ Sucking your toes
- ☛ Breakdancing
- ☛ Holding your breath until you pass out
- ☛ Going cross-eyed on purpose
- ☛ Thrusting your stomach out as far as it will go
- ☛ Plunging your finger in and out of your mouth with that knowing look

10 Things You Should Definitely Insist on When You Have a Vasectomy

- ◆ Anaesthetic
- ◆ Sterilised equipment
- ◆ A surgeon who doesn't bear a grudge against you
- ◆ A surgeon who's a real surgeon and not some loony in a white coat who wandered into the hospital off the street

◆ A surgeon who's done this operation before

◆ Only having the operation you went in for (e.g. not a sex change at the same time)

◆ A fresh scalpel

◆ The operating taking place in a proper operating theatre and not on a table in the staff canteen surrounded by half a dozen old cups of coffee and a sticky bun

◆ A surgeon who doesn't suffer from epilepsy

◆ Proper neat little stitches, not rivets, staples or a big bulldog clip

11 Stupid Things That Are Marginally Less Painful Than Natural Childbirth

☆ Getting Dawn French to stand on your foot

☆ Getting a paper cut in the little bit of webbed skin between your fingers and then pouring lemon juice over it

☆ Slamming your fingers in the front door

☆ Pouring boiling hot water through a funnel down your trousers

☆ Having your nipples pierced with a blunt pencil

☆ Feeding your feet into a paper shredder

☆ Rolling naked in a clump of stinging nettles

☆ Sticking a knitting needle in your eye

☆ Eating a cactus
☆ Having a full body wax by a beauty therapist who's new to the job
☆ Having a red-hot poker rammed up your bottom

10 People You Wouldn't Really Want to Give the Kiss of Life to

☨ Dr Hannibal Lecter
☨ Anyone with a great big herpe
☨ Anyone you really want to die
☨ The Elephant Man
☨ Nigel Lawson
☨ Your 80-year-old granny who's forgotten to wear her false teeth
☨ Anyone calling themselves Count Alucard
☨ Anyone who happens, for some reason or other, to have Superglue on their lips
☨ A big, beefy labourer
☨ Anyone who talks through their arse

JUST PLAIN STUPID

11 Lists You Hate to Compile

- People you owe money to
- All the things that your wife gets in the divorce settlement
- One night stands who might have got you pregnant
- All the words beginning with 'L'
- Reliable character witnesses for your forthcoming trial
- People to apologise to after last night
- Prices, part numbers and dimensions for mind-numbingly dull technical manuals that you have to do as part of your job
- Outstanding bills
- Things to do today
- Things you should've done today
- 11 lists you hate to compile

12 Words You Can Make Rude – Just by Changing One Letter!

- Walk
- Cant
- Funk
- Bus
- Pits
- Bum
- Tip
- Dock
- Ripples
- Bullocks
- Skunk
- Dingpiece

11 Things We Bet You're Not Doing While Reading This Book

- Lying next to Madonna in bed
- Lying next to Madonna anywhere else
- Orbiting the Earth in a Soviet space station
- Making an elaborate plan to kidnap Prince Harry
- Writing a thesis entitled *The Role of Sophisticated Satirical Literature in Late Twentieth-Century Society*
- Competing in the World Disco Dancing Championship
- Wishing you'd bought Maureen Lipman's book of British Telecom TV commercial scripts instead
- Defusing an unexploded WWII incendiary device
- Fighting Mike Tyson
- Performing a critical heart, liver and lung transplant operation
- Undergoing a critical heart, liver and lung transplant operation

5 Things We Bet You *Are* Doing While Reading This Book

- ☛ Scratching your head
- ☛ Standing in the bookshop
- ☛ Trying to look enthusiastic about receiving this book as a present in front of the person who bought it for you (try saying 'Yeah, it's great! It's just what I wanted! How did you know?')
- ☛ Number ones
- ☛ Number twos

13 Very Dark Colours

- ◆ Black
- ◆ Brilliant Black
- ◆ Light Black
- ◆ Midnight Black
- ◆ Royal Black
- ◆ Dark Black
- ◆ Navy Black
- ◆ Coal Black
- ◆ Pale Black
- ◆ Matt Black
- ◆ Peach Black
- ◆ *Noir Grand*
- ◆ Black with a Hint of Black

10 Things That Really Annoy Me About Mark Leigh, by his Wife, Debbie

- ☆ He decides he can't find what he's looking for, *before* he even looks
- ☆ He always leaves the lid of the biscuit tin just resting on it and not put back firmly
- ☆ He slurps drinks
- ☆ He sniffs *so* loudly
- ☆ He insists on putting the toilet roll on the

holder *the wrong way round* (i.e. with the loose end nearest the wall)

☆ The way he sucks peanuts into his mouth (it's *so* embarrassing)

☆ He doesn't speak into the mouthpiece when he's on the phone, making him difficult to hear

☆ He can't blow-dry his own hair

☆ He scratches his bottom when he's on the phone

☆ He made me stop this list at nine things

8 Very Big Numbers

✗ 10,548,639   ✗ 359,064,395
✗ 26,428,326   ✗ 996,481,063,491
✗ 155,328,749,552   ✗ 2,179,663,303
✗ 100,000,004   ✗ 43,159,612

9 Very Small Numbers

☀ 1   ☀ 1⅔   ☀ 2¹⁶⁄₁₉
☀ 3   ☀ 3¾   ☀ 1.2
☀ 2.3   ☀ 3.1   ☀ 1⅖

10 Occasions When It's Better *Not* to Be Naked

▦ Meeting your prospective in-laws for the first time

▦ Taking your cub scout troop out for a ramble

▦ A chance encounter with HM The Queen

▦ Giving the Sunday sermon

- When operating a bacon slicer
- Talking to your building society about a business loan
- When stopped in your car by the police
- In front of a mirror, just after finishing your Christmas dinner
- Appearing in court as a character witness for your best friend
- Anytime – if you're built like Bernard Manning

8 Songs for Manic Depressives

- ✕ 'I Die, You Die' – Gary Numan
- ✕ 'Crying' – Don McLean
- ✕ 'Little Willy' – Sweet
- ✕ 'King of Pain' – The Police
- ✕ 'Stop Your Sobbing' – The Pretenders
- ✕ The Sun Ain't Gonna Shine Anymore' – The Walker Brothers
- ✕ 'What Is Life' – Olivia Newton-John
- ✕ 'Seasons in the Sun' – Terry Jacks

18 Stupid Ways to Attempt to Get Into *The Guinness Book of Records*

- World record for bashing your head against something solid
- Fastest self-circumcision
- Longest period of abstinence from the toilet
- Most painful thing ever done to oneself
- Most car smashes

☛ Greatest electrical shock ever endured

☛ Most police officers head-butted in one evening

☛ Most laxatives consumed by one person

☛ Most stupid facial tattoo

☛ Longest period of walking in uncomfortable shoes

☛ Longest period of intercourse with an iguana

☛ Most spectacular suicide attempt

☛ Most live vipers swallowed in one hour

☛ Most rabid wolverines deposited down trousers in one hour

☛ Slowest recorded amble in the nude down Oxford Street

☛ Fastest loss of life savings on the horses

☛ Most time spent up to your neck in cowpats

☛ Most time spent listening to Dannii Minogue songs

10 Words Which We've Printed Upside Down

◆ Truce	◆ Jacobean
◆ Jollify	◆ Balaclava
◆ Invert	◆ Graceless
◆ Ululate	◆ Persona
◆ Rinse	◆ Dynamic

11 Things That Are Greasy

☆ Grease

☆ Fish and chips – if they're done properly

☆ Condoms
☆ Elvis Presley's pillowcase
☆ A Biro that's been dipped in butter
☆ The Uruguayan World Cup squad
☆ A gnu smeared with suntan lotion
☆ That ketchup stain on your best shirt
☆ A heavy metal fan's hair
☆ The cat's bottom in a Thai brothel
☆ Your hair, if you don't wash it for three
years

8 Stupid Things That Mark Leigh Once Bought

- ✗ A tie with a piano key design on it
- ✗ Another tie with a piano key design on it
- ✗ A big bar of Caramac, which he ate in one go
- ✗ A Yamaha XS250 (with wire wheels)
- ✗ Two years' worth of *Marvel Team Up* comics
- ✗ A ticket to see Arsenal play West Bromwich Albion at home in 1972
- ✗ Nik Kershaw's third album
- ✗ A Fiat X1/9

10 Words You Won't Find Anywhere Else in This Book, Except on This Page

- ☺ Zenith
- ☺ Aplomb
- ☺ Gala
- ☺ Misadventure
- ☺ Incognito
- ☺ Downgrade
- ☺ Tribulation
- ☺ Apocryphal
- ☺ Indiscretion
- ☺ Vociferous

2 Words Written in Morse Code That Look as Though They Might Be Rude But Which, In Fact, Are Not

10 Stupid things to Do with Spaghetti

✕ Thatch a cottage

✕ Do a very lacklustre impression of Bob Marley

✕ Scare your partner by pretending you have a tapeworm . . .

✕ Attempt to climb the Matterhorn, using spaghetti instead of rope

✕ Attach a scone to one end – and you'll have the world's first edible yo-yo!

✕ Indulge in very gentle games of bondage

✕ Try to hang yourself with a spaghetti noose

✕ Impress the girls by pulling it out of your wallet instead of cash

✕ Impress the girls by pulling it out of your flies

✕ Answer questions about it on *Mastermind*

10 Things About Mike Lepine That Irritate His Girlfriend, Philippa

☛ He goes to sleep with a notepad and pen in his hand when he's writing a book (and will suddenly sit up when I'm on the verge of sleep, shout something like 'Radiogram!' and start scribbling)

- He always manages to find the one thing I've forgotten to do in the flat
- He's usually right when he criticises me
- He wears his dressing gown when he's washing his hair, so that when *I* put it on, the collar and sleeves are wet
- He always gets a phone call during *Twin Peaks* or *Coronation Street*
- He kisses the dog hello before he kisses me
- He leaves cigarette ash in the bath
- He changes television channels every couple of minutes
- He forgets that I don't share his enthusiasm for Debbie Greenwood, Kate Bush, Beverley Craven, etc
- After watching a film, he starts to take on the characteristics of one of the main characters he's just seen – we are not going to watch *The Silence of the Lambs* or *Last Tango in Paris*.

7 Things Which Take a Lot of Stuffing

- A 400lb turkey
- A dead blue whale intended for a specimen case
- A duvet the size of Wales
- The British taxpayer
- A pillow which the whole human race could rest their heads on at night
- Son of Godzilla's teddy bear
- Clara Bow, if the stories are true . . .

10 Things with Holes in Them

☆ A Swiss cheese
☆ Doughnuts
☆ Iraqi servicemen
☆ Pierced nipples
☆ The plot of *Gremlins*
☆ The British legal system
☆ Pockets
☆ Jesus's hands
☆ Henry Moore sculptures
☆ Nuclear power-plant safety procedures

10 Things Which There Aren't Names for

✗	✗
✗	✗
✗	✗
✗	✗
✗	✗

15 Things You Don't Want to Find Yourself in *The Guinness Book of Records* for

☻ Loudest and longest death scream
☻ Person cheated on most often by their spouse
☻ Person cheated on with most partners by their spouse
☻ Person most often referred to as 'that complete dickhead'
☻ Longest recorded time spent on the lavatory by a human being
☻ Most useless person

- Ugliest Human Being of Modern Times
- Longest attack of hiccoughs
- Most underendowed male
- Highest plunge on to the face
- Longest time spent in an iron lung
- Biggest tosser
- Most recorded bones broken
- Worst dress sense
- Longest prison sentence served (unjustly)

10 Things You Wouldn't Want down Your Underpants

- A Malaysian bollock-eating lobster
- A lump of Number 4 reactor from Chernobyl
- A miniature working model of the guillotine bought as a souvenir to celebrate the bicentenary of the French Revolution
- The barrel of a sawn-off shotgun which just happens to have a dodgy safety catch
- A panicked shark
- 20 litres of Agent Orange
- Your treasured collection of used razor blades, some of which may have only been used for two shaves
- A bare copper wire, the other end of which is securely tied to a kite flying in a thunderstorm
- A bushel of stinging nettles
- Deep skidmarks

LAW AND ORDER

10 Stupid Things to do on Jury Service
- ✗ Openly accept a bribe from someone in the public gallery
- ✗ Wink knowingly at the defendant
- ✗ Shout 'Hanging's too good for him' and point at the defendant
- ✗ Shout 'Hanging's too good for him' and point at the judge
- ✗ Offer to take the place of the defendant
- ✗ Gob at the clerk of the court
- ✗ Claim £800 per day travelling expenses
- ✗ Shoot the defendant and say you believe in summary justice
- ✗ Inform the judge that you're an accomplice
- ✗ Wear Nazi uniform

10 Stupid Things to Demand During a Bank Robbery
- ☛ £25,000 in one-pence pieces
- ☛ £25,000 in marked notes

- A cheque for £25,000 made payable to yourself
- £5
- That you be locked in the vault and the police called
- A fluorescent green Reliant Robin as a getaway car
- Shorter working hours for people in the haberdashery business
- Anything beginning with 'X' (including a *xantippe* and a *xebec*)
- The location of El Dorado
- That only your good side be filmed on the hidden security cameras

10 Stupid Things to Say to a Policeman

- Oi, pig!
- Of course I've been drinking . . .
- Here's £3.50 to forget all about it
- Keep watch while I throw ammonia in the guard's face
- What about the Birmingham Six, eh?
- Your helmet looks like a giant prick
- Psssst! Interested in a Sony Nicam video recorder for sixty quid?
- I've got six ounces of illegal substances concealed up my arse
- You'll never take me alive, copper!
- I wish to make an official complaint about a police officer

10 Things You Don't Normally Associate with High Court Judges

☆ The song 'Young, Gifted and Black'

☆ Muscles

☆ Feminism

☆ Trendiness

☆ Tight stippled tigerskin posing pouches

☆ Comprehensive school educations

☆ Body popping

☆ Fingers on pulses

☆ Normal sexual behaviour

☆ Justice

8 People You Don't Want to Find Yourself Sharing a Cell with

☇ Some homicidal maniac who's violently claustrophobic

☇ Some hardcase who says you remind him of his girlfriend

☇ Some pervert who says you remind him of his dog

☇ Some headcase who says you remind him of his bathtub

☇ Anyone called Beefy Steve

☇ Anyone called Part-Them-Buns Benny

☇ Dr Hannibal Lecter

☇ Bruce Forsyth

10 Stupid Crimes to Specialise in
☺ Stealing library books
☺ Robbing gumball machines
☺ Suicide
☺ Selling your body for money
☺ Using crack
☺ Pointing the wrong way when people ask you directions
☺ Incest
☺ Failing to curb your dog
☺ Writing scripts for *Emmerdale Farm*
☺ Spitting on public transport

10 Stupid Ways to Disguise Yourself Prior to Committing a Criminal Act
▪ Change your shoes
▪ Wear your coat inside out
▪ Smear yourself with boot polish (or whitewash)
▪ Wear a striped jersey and mask, and carry a sack with 'swag' stencilled on it
▪ Slash your face with a razor to create a prominent scar
▪ Cut off an arm so that the police will think a one-armed man committed the crime
▪ Put on 150lb so that the police will be looking for an obese criminal
▪ Dress up as the Pope, because no one will suspect the Pope of committing the crime

- Wear a giant penguin suit, so that the police will be convinced the witnesses must be mistaken
- Disguise yourself as *yourself*, so that you can claim you were framed

11 Stupid Ways to Try to Become Totally Ruthless, Undisputed Master of the World

- ✗ Ask nicely
- ✗ Run for high office in Papua New Guinea
- ✗ Find a steady job and hope to work your way up through the ranks to Master of the World
- ✗ Try to take over the world when there's nobody looking
- ✗ Tell everyone that you're the Master of the World – and hope they'll believe you
- ✗ Threaten to have a temper tantrum unless you get world power
- ✗ Make a cash offer for it
- ✗ Disguise yourself as the Master of the World – and hope everyone falls for it
- ✗ Attempt to win the world in a lottery
- ✗ Replace all the world's leaders with android doubles who are under your complete control
- ✗ Marry the Totally Ruthless, Undisputed Mistress of the World

9 Things High Court Judges Don't Listen To

- ☛ Radio 1
- ☛ *Thomas the Tank Engine* stories, read by Ringo Starr
- ☛ Metallica
- ☛ Stupid *women*
- ☛ Doctors who told them 15 years ago that their brains were going
- ☛ That wee small voice inside that says 'You're talking nonsense'
- ☛ Their hearts
- ☛ Public opinion
- ☛ Reason

10 Stupid Last Requests on Death Row

- ◆ To hear 'Wombling Merry Christmas' one last time
- ◆ To have a Big Mac & fries for your last meal
- ◆ To go an hour early
- ◆ To make a dinner reservation for next weekend
- ◆ To sleep with Barbara Cartland
- ◆ To consult an insurance salesman
- ◆ To visit the dentist
- ◆ To have Sir Harry Secombe's autograph
- ◆ To meet Rolf Harris in the flesh
- ◆ A calendar

LOVE, SEX AND MARRIAGE

14 Stupid Things to Put in a Lonely Hearts Ad if You're a Man

☆ Premature ejaculation

☆ Austin Allegro owner

☆ Destitute

☆ Compulsive smoker, drinker and gambler

☆ Transvestite

☆ Insurance salesman

☆ Acne-ridden

☆ Contagious

☆ 8 children from a previous marriage

☆ Truly obese

☆ Wife beater

☆ Panties

☆ Pervert

☆ Con artist

11 Stupid Chat-Up Lines

- ✗ Hi, I've got a small penis
- ✗ I'm unemployed with no money, no job prospects and terminal BO
- ✗ Hey dollface, ever been for a ride in a Skoda Favorit before?
- ✗ I wonder what your head would look like on a stick
- ✗ Do you want to come back to my place and see my Hornby OO scale model railway?
- ✗ I bet you've never met someone with as many contagious sexually transmitted diseases as me
- ✗ Anyway, there I was, talking to Ian Brady when who should come into the room but my old mate Dennis Nilsen . . .
- ✗ Has anyone ever told you that you look just like Michelle from *Eastenders*?
- ✗ If my friend over there said you had a beautiful body, would you hold it against him?
- ✗ So there I was, on my yacht in Monte Carlo when . . . oooops! . . . oh shit! There I go again – filling up my incontinence pants . . .
- ✗ Zebra jam jar china orange balloon wheeeeeeeeeeeeeeee!!!

13 Things You Don't Want to Hear from the Girl You've Just Taken Home with You

- ☺ I have to get up early for work tomorrow
- ☺ I suddenly feel very tired
- ☺ I like you as a friend
- ☺ I can feel my period starting
- ☺ I'm a virgin and you'll have to marry me first
- ☺ Does this mean we're engaged?
- ☺ I feel like talking
- ☺ Call it women's intuition, but I know you couldn't hope to satisfy me
- ☺ I've changed my mind
- ☺ Do me a favour and fuck off
- ☺ All that drink you've been plying me with has gone straight to my head. I'm going to be sick.
- ☺ Of course the courts cleared me. They said I did it in my sleep, you see . . .
- ☺ My last boyfriend had eleven inches. I can't wait to see how you measure up

10 Dangerous Places to Make Love

- On the runway in front of an El-Al jumbo taxiing for take off
- In the fast lane of the M4
- In the holiest of Muslim shrines
- In the back seat of a car gripped in the junkyard car crusher
- In front of her husband

- 🔒 Surrounded by highly volatile nitroglycerine
- 🔒 On a beach thronged with flesh-eating scavenger crabs
- 🔒 On the beach near Sellafield
- 🔒 In a vat of concentrated sulphuric acid
- 🔒 Thailand

10 Stupid Ways to Revive the Novelty in Your Sex Life

✕ The man dresses up as Catwoman, while his lover dresses up as Pitt the Elder

✕ The woman spanks herself with a ping-pong bat while the man takes Polaroids

✕ The man smears himself with loganberry jam while the woman goes to the cinema

✕ The man ties himself up to the ironing board, while the woman pelts him with Cheesy Wotsits

✕ The woman sellotapes a feather duster to her bottom while her partner brings himself to orgasm with a copy of *Homes and Gardens*

✕ The man chews pieces of Wrigley's Juicy Fruit gum, which he then sticks to each of his partner's erogenous zones in turn

✕ The woman uses processed cheese slices to deviant effect, while her partner crimps her hair and recites John Hegley poetry

✕ Both partners sit in the cupboard under the stairs and thrash each other with stinging nettles

✕ The woman rubs her partner's body with a Nigel Kennedy CD, while the man cracks his knuckles

✕ The couple make love in time to Val Doonican's 'Paddy McGinty's Goat'

13 Stupid Places to Try and Find Your Mr Right

❤ Broadmoor

❤ A Soho peepshow

❤ Woolworth's

❤ Standing on a cold station platform, taking down numbers

❤ Shopping in Millets

❤ Yelling at you from the building site

❤ A VD clinic

❤ A boy scout jamboree

❤ The maternity ward of your local hospital

❤ At a Megadeth concert

❤ At a Communards concert

❤ Bringing you your Brown Derby at the Wimpy

❤ Tehran

10 Stupid Gifts to Give Your Girlfriend on Valentine's Day

🖛 A framed signed photograph of Kate Bush

🖛 A framed signed photograph of you with your ex-girlfriend

☛ A credit card

☛ Some soap, extra-strong deodorant and a powerful oral hygiene mouthwash

☛ A size 16 dress (when you know full well she's size 14 and sensitive about it)

☛ Sexy undies

☛ A film entitled *Lesbians of Mars*

☛ Nose-hair clippers

☛ A £1 Woolworth's token

☛ Crabs

10 Stupid Ways to Fake Orgasm

◆ Bash your head repeatedly against the headboard, gasping *'Je t'aime . . . je t'aime . . .'*

◆ Bounce off all four corners of the room, doing your impression of a steam locomotive

◆ Say, 'Oh, I've come . . . ', rather matter-of-factly

◆ Run out of the room screaming, 'Yesohyesohyesohyes!!'

◆ Beat your breast and yodel like Tarzan

◆ Roll off the bed and keep rolling over and over, whispering, *'So good . . . so good . . .'*

◆ Vibrate violently while conjugating a common Latin verb

◆ Throw salad cream everywhere and say, 'Well, that's it . . .'

◆ Grip your partner's sexual organs as tightly as you can, pretending to be lost in the throes of rapture

◆ Pretend to be unconscious for such an extraordinary length of time that your partner panics and calls an ambulance

2 Stupid Tell-Tale Signs That a Man's a Virgin

☆ He says he is

☆ He says he isn't

10 Stupid Words or Phrases You Wouldn't Want Your Best Man to Use in His Speech

✗ Recent sex-change operation

✗ 3-month suspended sentence

✗ Biggest mistake of his life

✗ Syphilis

✗ Gay lover

✗ Biggest slapper in the school

✗ Crap in bed

✗ Virgin

✗ I'd give them three months

✗ Boils

12 Stupid Brand Names for Condoms

☼ Eensy Weensy™	☼ Micro™
☼ Insensitivo™	☼ Splitters™
☼ Petite™	☼ Crappy™
☼ Easi-Break™	☼ Sphincter-Safe™

❋ Detumescencers™ ❋ John-Paul
❋ Black Premmies™   Minilites™
❋ Leakies™

14 Stupid Pet Names for Your Wife or Girlfriend

⬛ Whore Slave
⬛ My Cuddly Warthog
⬛ Dog's Breath
⬛ Dirt Box
⬛ Flatsie
⬛ Fatso
⬛ Vermin Skunk Face
⬛ Snivelling Toad
⬛ *Ma Petite Cochon*
⬛ Farty
⬛ Jumbo Thighs
⬛ Thick Cow
⬛ Haemorrhoid Features
⬛ Frankenstein's Ringpiece

The 10 Most Stupid Items to Use to Set the Mood for an Intimate Evening in

✗ Picture-book of Vietnamese war atrocities

✗ Bucket of steaming cat entrails underneath a glass-topped coffee table

✗ Your CD of Stuka dive-bomber sound effects

✗ Album of press cuttings about your sex-change operation

✗ Wax effigy of your date with pins stuck in it

✗ Copy of *American Psycho* with all the good bits underlined and 'Yes!' scrawled in the margins

- ✕ Huge pentangle burned into the carpet
- ✕ Your spare false leg propped up against the wall, near the door
- ✕ Framed photographs of your previous 17 partners
- ✕ Framed photographs of your previous 17 big jobs

10 Stupid Things to Do if You're Trying to Get Pregnant

- ♥ Run away to a convent
- ♥ Shut your partner's private parts in the door
- ♥ Keep taking the highest dosage oestrogen pill
- ♥ Insist on safe sex
- ♥ Date a eunuch
- ♥ Superglue your fallopian tubes shut
- ♥ Have sex within a mile of Sellafield
- ♥ Douche with industrial strength spermicide
- ♥ Celebrate your 70th birthday
- ♥ Stay faithful to your lesbian lover

11 Stupid Things to Say if Your Boyfriend or Husband Catches You in Bed with a Rhinoceros

- ☛ Oh God! I thought you were still at the office
- ☛ It's not what you think
- ☛ I've been meaning to tell you about this for some time

☛ I was feeling a bit horny

☛ . . . And furthermore, he's Wayne and Cindy's real father!

☛ I just woke up and there he was

☛ Darling, you remember my friend Thelma, don't you . . .

☛ Rhinoceros? What rhinoceros?

☛ Let me tell you, he's ten times the mammal you'll ever be!

☛ It's a fair cop; he wouldn't fit in the wardrobe

☛ How do you like my nifty new pyjama case?

10 Stupid Things to Mention When You First Meet the Person of Your Dreams

◆ Your stamp collection

◆ Your 12-month battle against crab infestation

◆ Hard bondage

◆ Albanian socio-political theory

◆ Your 25 yards breaststroke certificate

◆ The tube of Preparation H you always carry with you

◆ Bogies

◆ Your verruca

◆ The somewhat unusual mating habits of the common anteater

◆ That they're the person of your dreams . . .

15 Songs for Perverts

☆ 'Love Me, Love My Dog' by Peter Shelley

☆ '7 Little Girls Sitting in the Back Seat' by The Avons

☆ 'Automatic Lover' by Dee D. Jackson

☆ 'A Boy Named Sue' by Johnny Cash

☆ 'Hello Dolly' by Louis Armstrong

☆ 'Dress You Up' by Madonna

☆ 'One Night in Bangkok' by Murray Head

☆ 'Goodbye Sam, Hello Samantha' by Cliff Richard

☆ 'Hurts So Good' by Susan Cadogan

☆ 'Good Vibrations' by The Beach Boys

☆ 'Istanbul' by Frankie Vaughan

☆ 'Little Donkey' by Nina and Frederick

☆ 'Do You Really Want to Hurt Me' by Culture Club

☆ 'Experiments with Mice' by Johnny Dankworth

☆ 'Tie Your Mother Down' by Queen

The 10 Most Stupid Things to Say to Your Wife When She Suspects You're Having an Affair with Another Woman

⚲ Hello darling. Guess what, I'm having an affair!

⚲ Goodnight darling, I'm just going off to sleep with my mistress

✴ Not tonight, darling, I only had it off at lunchtime . . .

✴ While I'm out, if someone called Sally rings, tell her I'll slip out to meet her as soon as you've gone to sleep

✴ Slip this basque on. It looked like dynamite on Lisa, so it should be OK on you too . . .

✴ Darling, I've got to fly to Verona on business. Do you know where the condoms are?

✴ Darling, I'm just going to take the dog out for a walk. Have you seen my clean underwear?

✴ I just thought it was about time I started wearing aftershave again, that's all . . .

✴ Sharon never complains!

✴ Cop a load of these lovebites!

Andrea and Tim's Wedding Guest List

☀ Lorraine
☀ Nathan
☀ John
☀ Tony
☀ Tracy
☀ The twins
☀ Baby Ben
☀ Philippa
☀ Mike
☀ Nana
☀ Pop
☀ Two of Tim's friends
☀ Sharon
☀ Mum
☀ Dad

10 Stupid Words and Phrases Used in Pornographic Magazines that *Nobody* Ever Uses in Real Life

- Manhood
- Porridge gun
- Swollen love bud
- 'Feed me your meat . . .'
- Fierce tonguing
- Plump love lips
- Mound
- Up it went for the third time . . .
- Nine incher
- My luxury apartment

10 Stupid Ways to Get Anyone You Ever Wanted Into Bed with You

(If we knew this we wouldn't bother writing this stupid book)

13 Things You Wouldn't Want Your Wife to Take on Honeymoon with Her

- ✕ Your best man
- ✕ A chastity belt
- ✕ A comprehensive listing of when all the ships are due in port
- ✕ Her lesbian lover
- ✕ A pair of industrial bolt cutters and a thick leather strap to bite on
- ✕ Four 15,000-piece jigsaws
- ✕ A pregnancy testing kit

✘ 2-week supply of tampons

✘ Her signed vow of celibacy

✘ The business card of a top divorce lawyer

✘ A monster jar of anti-thrush ointment

✘ Two Turkish musclemen

✘ Her mother

10 Stupid Items of Clothing to Get Your Girlfriend to Dress up in, to Spice up Your Sex Life

♥ Horsehair blanket

♥ Thick argyle sweater and matching mittens

♥ NASA space suit

♥ The national dress of Greenland

♥ Suit of armour

♥ Anything that makes her look like Judi Dench

♥ Anything that makes her look 4 stone heavier

♥ A brown anorak

♥ A boy scout outfit

♥ Sou'wester and oilskins

10 Stupid Ways to Leave Your Lover

☛ Via a tunnel you've secretly been digging, concealed beneath the sofa

☛ Out of the window with an ex-NASA jet pack strapped to your back

☛ In a bubble car with the stereo blasting out 'Good to Be Back' by Gary Glitter

- In a wooden glider constructed from old packing cases and rafters that you've been building in the loft
- On a space hopper
- In a dustbin that you've been hiding in, outside her house
- Fired from a giant cannon, with a crash helmet strapped to your head
- Surreptitiously, disguised as the back end of a pantomime horse
- On a Sinclair C5
- In a coffin, after you've been shot dead by her jealous husband

19 Things You Don't Want Your Girlfriend to Find in Your Flat

- Luscious Lucy, the blow-up doll with *real hair* and revolving tonsils
- *Mein Kampf*
- 25 feet of coiled rope and a ski mask
- Your other girlfriend
- Those underpants you meant to wash in 1987, but keep leaving on the draining board
- A rhinoceros
- Julian Clary, who's innocently popped round to borrow a cup of sugar
- Your stash of pervy mags
- Your stash of sodden Kleenex
- Two packets of Ejaculex 2000 pills

- That love poem you wrote to Dannii Minogue when you were pissed
- A large bottle of gangrene liniment
- An electric cattle prod
- That pair of saucy girl's knickers your mates have hidden in your flat for a laugh
- A photograph of Rock Hudson, signed 'Thanks for last night . . .'
- A truss with 4" nails banged into it
- Pages torn from a children's underwear catalogue
- A well-thumbed book entitled *How to Please a Woman in Bed*
- Dennis Norden's *Bumper Book of Chat-Up Lines*

9 Things You Don't Want Your Boyfriend to Find in Your Flat

- ☆ Tickets to see The Chippendales
- ☆ A naked Chippendale
- ☆ That personal reply from Claire Rayner advising you to ditch him . . . and seek specialist legal (and/or medical) advice
- ☆ A well-thumbed copy of *How to Improve Your Man in Bed*
- ☆ Indisputable evidence that you're sleeping with the population of Truro behind his back
- ☆ That photograph of you the school photographer took when you were ten

☆ A massive luminous vibrating stippled artificial penis

☆ That jumbo tube of Preparation H you keep forgetting to put away

☆ That picture of Mel Gibson you've covered in lipstick kisses

10 Stupid Things You Shouldn't Do Immediately Before Making Love

⚥ Groin yourself with an iron bar

⚥ Drink four pints of Horlicks

⚥ Run a mini-marathon (or even up the stairs too vigorously)

⚥ Tell your partner you've just slept with their best friend

⚥ Smear yourself from head to toe with garlic butter

⚥ Plunge your hands and feet into a bucket of dry ice

⚥ Read a book called *Pubic Lice – The Hidden Menace*

⚥ Discover that 'she' is really a he – called Dave

⚥ Look at pictures of King Dong

⚥ Look at yourself in the mirror

13 Songs It Would Be Stupid to Have Played as You Walk down the Aisle . . .

☺ 'D.I.V.O.R.C.E'

☺ 'You're Having My Baby'

☺ 'It's All Over Now'

☻ 'Crying in the Chapel'

☻ 'Please Release Me'

☻ 'Glad to Be Gay'

☻ 'Walk Away Renee'

☻ 'I Want to Break Free'

☻ 'Love Don't Live Here Anymore'

☻ 'So Many Women, So Little Time . . . '

☻ 'We Gotta Get Out of This Place . . . '

☻ 'It's Raining Men'

☻ 'Gin Gan Goolie'

10 Stupid Ways to Discover You're Really a Pervert

☐ You're watching *All Creatures Great and Small* – and you suddenly realise that you've got an erection

☐ You're watching Bruce Forsyth – and you suddenly realise you've got an erection

☐ You're watching *Kate Bush – The Videos*, and you suddenly realise you *don't* have an erection

☐ You're sharing an intimate candlelit dinner for two – with an Alsatian in a tutu

☐ You've got more erotic underwear than she has

☐ You suddenly can't pass a traffic cone without giving in to the urge to impale yourself on it

▣ You check your wife's birth certificate –
   and discover that she's really your long-
   lost sister
▣ You go to Turkey for your holidays – and
   suddenly feel like you're coming home
▣ You accidentally pierce your scrotal sac
   with a soldering iron – and it feels
   sooooooo good . . .
▣ You catch yourself flirting with the
   vegetables

10 Stupid (But Apt) Titles for Pornographic Magazines

✕ *All-Colour Tosspot!*

✕ *Sexist Crap!*

✕ *Inadequates' Monthly*

✕ *Jerk-Off Pocket Digest!*

✕ *Mr Masturbator (Pour l'Homme)*

✕ *Totally Unreal Sex Objects on Parade!*

✕ *Diddle!*

✕ *Pocket Billiards International*

✕ *Sad Lonely Men Only*

✕ *Stroke!*

HEAVENS ABOVE!

10 Stupid Names That Adam and Eve Might Have Been Called, Had the Bible Been Written Today

- Kevin and Sharon
- Darren and Tracey
- Gary and Lisa
- Mick and Sandra
- Errol and Cath
- Martin and Angie
- Vince and Tina
- Eric and Mabel
- Steve and Elaine
- Terry and June

---

1 Creature That Noah Probably Regretted Putting in His Ark

- ◆ Woodworm

---

10 Things You Definitely Don't Want to Be Reincarnated as

- ☆ A tapeworm
- ☆ A dung beetle
- ☆ A tick
- ☆ Cecil Parkinson's love child

☆ A backward amoeba

☆ A Belgian

☆ An Iranian girl-child

☆ A pit bull terrier

☆ Something that ends up in pet food

☆ Yourself, probably

20 of the Many Things That Angels of the Lord Do Not Do

🕆 Organise themselves into soccer teams

🕆 Play with themselves

🕆 Praise the Lord with smutty little rugby ditties

🕆 Appear when you need them

🕆 Tell Jesus jokes

🕆 Drink real ale

🕆 Collect plane numbers

🕆 Play hoop-la with their halos

🕆 Play Knock Down Ginger

🕆 Appear on *Blind Date*

🕆 Play 'Sweet Child of Mine' on their harps

🕆 Play electric guitars and drums instead of harps

🕆 Shoot up with smack

🕆 Pinch the bottom of the angel next to them in the choir invisible

🕆 Pervy things with cherubs

🕆 Expose themselves to nuns

🕆 Burp

✗ Moon passing airliners

✗ Fetch Indian takeaways for the Lord

✗ Snigger and nudge each other every time someone says, 'The coming of the Lord is nigh!'

Stupid Subjects for Sunday Sermons

☀ Bird's Eye boil-in-a-bag meals

☀ Julia Roberts's legs

☀ The lifespan of the emu

☀ *Only Fools and Horses*

☀ Big jobs

☀ Cough linctus

☀ Who'll be number one in the charts next week

☀ Key fobs

☀ The benefits of atheism

☀ Harold Pinter

10 Things Which We Hope There Won't Be in the Afterlife

▣ Cricket

▣ Constipation

▣ Bingo nights

▣ Folk music

▣ Too much religion

▣ Square dancing

▣ Babies who cry all night forever

🛍 Nowhere to park

🛍 Bloody choirs everywhere

🛍 Benny Hill in cabaret – every night

12 Things Which We Hope There *Will* Be in the Afterlife

✗ Sex

✗ Bell's whisky

✗ Jukeboxes (and change for them)

✗ Ferrari Testarossas for everyone

✗ Raucous parties that you don't remember a thing about the day after

✗ A branch of the Halifax (so we *can* take it with us . . .)

✗ Comfy beds

✗ Kinky underwear

✗ Blondes

✗ Pubs

✗ Cream cakes made of manna with no calories

✗ Amazonian women who just won't take no for an answer

11 Things That God Frowns Upon You Praying for

☛ £1 million in untraceable used notes

☛ Rosanna Arquette and a vat of semolina

☛ Four extra inches

- ☛ The New Kids on the Block tour bus to be in simultaneous collision with six petrol tankers and a lorry carrying high explosives
- ☛ A new Maserati
- ☛ A Rolex
- ☛ The off-licence still to be open
- ☛ Fine weather for the second test
- ☛ A large tax error in your favour
- ☛ Unimaginable violence descending upon your boss
- ☛ Proof

10 Stupid Ways to Try and Trick Your Way Through the Pearly Gates, if St Peter Refuses to Let You in

- ◆ Avon calling!
- ◆ A package for Mr God . . .
- ◆ Jehovah's Witnesses! (They'll pretend to be out)
- ◆ I've come to read the meter . . .
- ◆ Is this the party? I'm a mate of John's . . .
- ◆ I'm a vet. I hear you've got an angel in there with wing moult . . .
- ◆ I'm from the local council. We're doing this survey . . .
- ◆ My car's broken down. Can I use your phone, please?
- ◆ I've come to give the cherabim their singing lessons
- ◆ I'm from SKY TV's *Search for a Star*, come to audition the choir invisible . . .

28 Entertainers Named After Characters in the Bible

☆ MADONNA

☆ Curtis and ISHMAEL

☆ Chris ISAAK

☆ ESTHER Rantzen

☆ MARY Hopkin

☆ David JACOBs

☆ JOSEPH Bottoms

☆ JESSE Matthews

☆ MARK Hamill

☆ MIRIAM Karlin

☆ JOHN Sessions

☆ LUKE and MATTHEW Goss (from Bros)

☆ PAUL Young

☆ SARAH Brightman

☆ MICHAEL CAINe

☆ BENJAMIN Britten

☆ DEBORAH Harry

☆ DANIEL Day-Lewis

☆ Father ABRAHAM and the Smurfs

☆ RUTH Maddock

☆ ADAM West

☆ JONATHAN Ross

☆ EVE Graham (of New Seekers fame)

☆ Peter GABRIEL

☆ DAVID Essex

☆ RACHEL Ward

☆ Yannick NOAH (a tennis player,
apparently)
☆ GODley & Creme

11 Occasions on Which You Don't Want the Virgin Mary Suddenly to Appear Unto You

☥ While walking a tightrope over Niagara
Falls

☥ During your psychiatric evaluation

☥ Just when you're trying to convince your
wife that you haven't got another woman
in the house

☥ Just as you're about to bring your jumbo
jet in to land at Heathrow

☥ While indulging in a furtive wank

☥ Just after you've given the Pope the finger

☥ Just as you're in the process of applying
some Preparation H . . .

☥ When you're shaving off your pubic hair
with a cutthroat razor

☥ While attempting to summon up the devil

☥ While dressing up in your wife's clothes
and parading up and down in front of the
mirror

☥ While interfering with barnyard fowl

12 Stupid Places for the Second Coming to Occur

☀ On the moon

☀ Outside Burger King

☀ Inside Britain's largest mental hospital

☀ Between two slices of bread

☀ Inside a small septic tank

☀ Behind your skirting board

☀ At a midnight showing of *The Life of Brian*

☀ In your bedroom just when you're trying to get to sleep

☀ In a patch of quicksand

☀ In the fast lane of the M1

☀ Glasgow on a Saturday night

☀ Milton Keynes (any time)

10 Things Which the Bible Fails to Give Us Any Guidance on

▣ If Adam and Eve were the first people, then who did Cain marry?

▣ Who was God's dad?

▣ Why do we always seem to get cramp at that vital moment?

▣ How to be an incredible lover

▣ Who's the better singer – Whitney Houston or Janet Jackson?

▣ Making quiche Lorraine

▣ What to make of Su Pollard

▣ Why there is a Milton Keynes

▣ How to get a recording contract

▣ Does Stork margarine really taste like butter?

10 People You Probably Won't See in Heaven

✗ Attila the Hun

✗ Minicab drivers

✗ Anyone in the Nazi party

✗ Anyone in the Conservative party

✗ Anyone who was involved with, or went to see *The Life of Brian*

✗ Anyone who's laughed at a rude joke in this book

✗ Anyone who's shoplifted this book

✗ Our publisher

✗ Any other publisher

✗ Us

11 Gifts That the Baby Jesus Would Have Wanted Instead of Gold, Frankincense and Myrrh if He Were Alive Today

☛ Nintendo Game Boy

☛ Walkman with auto reverse and 3-band graphic equaliser

☛ Mountain bike

☛ Walkie-talkie set

☛ Radio-controlled model jeep

☛ £30 record token

☛ 8mm camcorder

☛ Tasty trainers

☛ Set of all the *Nightmare on Elm Street* videos

☛ Laptop computer

☛ 'Le Mans' Scalextric set

11 Stupid Things You Never See People Do on *Songs of Praise*

◆ Proudly hold a burning cross
◆ Sing rude words to the tune of 'Jerusalem'
◆ Read unsavoury literature hidden behind their hymn books
◆ Fart to the tune of *He Who Would Valiant Be*
◆ Pick their nose and flick it
◆ Wear a goat's-head mask
◆ Look as though they're really having a good time
◆ Wave at the camera and do V-signs behind the head of the person sitting in the pew in front
◆ Hold up a placard saying 'Hello Mum'
◆ Hold up a placard saying 'Hello Heavenly Father'
◆ Look younger than 63

10 Stupid Things That Nuns Never Do

☆ Drink 8 cans of Special Brew after lights out
☆ Read dirty mags
☆ Arm-wrestle for money
☆ Arm-wrestle for the hell of it
☆ Take it in turns to have wild sex with the gardener behind the potting shed
☆ Draw rude pictures of Mother Teresa

☆ Blaspheme using sign language
☆ Wear open-crotch panties and red silk basques
☆ Get tattooed
☆ Press-ups in the cucumber patch (despite the rumours)

12 Plagues That Moses Could Have Smitten the Egyptians with

✗ The plague of hair on the palms of your hands so that people look at you funny
✗ The plague of the firstborn destined to grow up to become hairdressers and choreographers
✗ The plague of crocodiles nesting in your girdle
✗ The plague of being right next door to Libya
✗ The plague of beautiful maidens who are only interested in your money
✗ The plague of just missing the chariot to work and having to wait half an hour for the next one to come along
✗ The plague of running out of eggs just when you *really* fancy an omelette
✗ The plague of itchy groins in public
✗ The plague of head colds that just won't go away, no matter how much orange juice you drink
✗ The plague of hair that you can't do a thing with

✴ The plague of not being able to get a date on Friday night

✴ The plague of 40-foot pubic lice

14 Things It Would Be *Very* Stupid for the Pope to Do

☉ Walk around with a huge black panther straining at the leash

☉ Snigger every time he says, 'You may kiss my ring'

☉ Hit himself on the head with a mallet

☉ Do wheelies on a top-of-the-range Harley

☉ Get someone pregnant

☉ Rip all his clothes off and run shrieking through St Peter's

☉ Record a duet with Madonna

☉ Come out of the closet

☉ Tell everyone it's all been a big hoax . . .

☉ Declare that, henceforth, he wishes to be known as 'Lucille'

☉ Drive the Popemobile in a demolition derby

☉ Appear in a Mates commercial

☉ Lose his faith

☉ Use the Turin Shroud to wipe his bottom

10 Headlines You're Extremely Unlikely to See in *The War Cry*

▣ WAS JESUS A SPACE ALIEN?

▣ HOLY TRINITY IN BIZARRE LOVE TRIANGLE

- 5000 CANS OF SPECIAL BREW MUST BE WON INSIDE!
- MALE SALVATIONIST GIVES BIRTH TO TWO-HEADED ALIEN BABY
- LIMBLESS MISSIONARY MARRIES AFRICAN PYGMY CONVERT!
- WAS WILLIAM BOOTH A WOMAN?
- HEAVEN FOUND – IN ILFORD!
- SALVATION ARMY MARCHING BAND FOUND ON MARS!
- IT'S OFFICIAL! SALLY ARMY CAPTAINS MAKE BETTER LOVERS!
- INSIDE: PLAY 'SPOT THE SINNER' . . . AND WIN, WIN, WIN!

10 Stupid Things to Give up for Lent

✗ Breathing

✗ Your religious beliefs

✗ Fellatio

✗ Incredible wealth

✗ Fast cars

✗ Well-endowed women

✗ Jaffa cakes

✗ Getting a seat on crowded trains

✗ Staying up late watching dirty videos and drinking beer with the lads

✗ Going to the toilet

10 Sensible Things to Give up for Lent

- Venture scouting
- Paying tax, national insurance and VAT
- Chastity
- Sex with marsupials
- Watching *Bob's Your Uncle*
- Matt Bianco LPs
- Train spotting
- Alimony payments
- Going to the dentist
- Having anything whatsoever to do with lawyers

10 Stupid Names for Salvation Army Soup Kitchens Which Want to Appear Chic

- Hobo's
- Bumm's of Covent Garden
- Wino's
- The Little Tramp
- Dosser's of Berwick Street
- Monsieur Vagrant
- Dine 'n' Out
- The Hard Luck Cafe
- Itinerenti
- Chez Box

THE GRACIOUS WORLD OF ROYALTY

10 Words and Phrases You'll Never Hear in the Queen's Christmas Speech

☆ Git

☆ Nice to see you, to see you, nice

☆ I bet my TV set is better than the one you're watching on, matey

☆ So there I was, naked as the day I was born . . .

☆ Bitch

☆ Scum

☆ Hereditary madness runs in our family

☆ Did you hear the one about . . .

☆ Anyway, I get loads more money than any of you plebs watching . . .

☆ So I urge you all to storm the palace and instigate a revolution

8 People Who Sound Like They May Be Relatives of the Queen (But Aren't)

✘ Prince

✘ Count Basie

✘ Jack Lord

✘ Martin Luther King

✘ Duke Ellington

✘ Steve McQueen

✘ The Baron Knights

✘ Dame Edna Everage

10 Types of People the Queen Simply Hates to Meet During Walkabouts

☀ People who smell

☀ People who drop their aitches and talk like oiks

☀ People who want to give her a big sloppy wet kiss

☀ People after a hot racing tip

☀ People who say, 'I thought you'd be taller . . .' or 'Haven't you grown old?'

☀ Louts who want her to autograph their bottoms

☀ Commoners who shout 'Liz!' or 'Queenie!'

☀ People who want her to pose next to someone, with her arm around them

☀ People who say, 'You look much better on the stamps . . .'

☀ People who ask her tricky questions like 'What do you think of Fergie?', 'Is Charles really loopy?' or 'Name the two stars of *Another 48 Hours*'

17 Methods of Transportation That the Queen Will Not Normally Use to Get to Her Public Engagements

- Tube train
- 2000 hp nitro-burning dragster
- Roller-skates
- Skateboard
- Sitting astride a donkey
- Ex-NASA jet pack
- Sprinting as fast as she can
- Rickshaw
- Hitching a lift on approaches to the motorway
- No. 42 bus
- Hang-glider
- Go-cart
- Pogo-stick
- A chariot with scythes on the wheels
- Stilts
- Space hopper
- A piggy-back from HRH Prince Philip

12 Women We *Guarantee* Prince Edward Will Not Take For His Bride

- ✕ Joan Collins
- ✕ Prunella Scales
- ✕ Tessa Sanderson
- ✕ Madonna
- ✕ Whitney Houston
- ✕ Joan Jett
- ✕ Dame Edna Everage
- ✕ Tula
- ✕ Maria Whittaker
- ✕ Fatima Whitbread
- ✕ Lynne Perrie (*Coronation Street*'s Ivy Tilsley)
- ✕ Anyone *you* know

11 Things That Andy and Fergie Get up to in Bed

- ☛ Eating snacks
- ☛ Farting contests under the blankets
- ☛ Games of Hunt the Crumbs
- ☛ Joking about all those who had to get up *hours* ago . . .
- ☛ A competition to see who can drink the most champagne, do the loudest burp and then pass out for 48 hours
- ☛ Throwing biscuits at the TV set when a Labour politician comes on
- ☛ Giggly food fights
- ☛ Who can pull the funniest face competitions
- ☛ Arguments about who's going to call the servants to bring more champagne and biscuits

☛ Flicking lumps of caviar up at the ceiling and seeing if they stick

☛ Various games that Andy learned in the Navy

Prince William's Christmas List
◆ Everything

6 Things Prince Charles Hates to Be Asked
☆ Are those ears real or are you wearing them for a bet?

☆ Do you think you'll be too old by the time you get a shot at the throne?

☆ Are you completely out to lunch?

☆ Is it really all over between you and her indoors?

☆ Why do you talk like that?

☆ When are you going to be king, then?

10 Names Prince Charles Hates to Be Called
✗ Chazza	✗ Baldy
✗ Chuck	✗ The Big C
✗ Dumbo	✗ Chucky-poos
✗ Lugs	✗ Big Ears
✗ Charlie-baby	✗ Jug Handles

10 Reasons to Retain the Monarchy
☀ Old ladies and foreigners seem to quite like them

☀ They're good for a laugh

- ☻ While Fergie's living in splendour, she's not living next door to you
- ☻ Someone has to defend us against the threat of being overrun by dangerous grouse, deer and foxes
- ☻ We owe it to them for inspiring a great TV show like *The Munsters*
- ☻ If the monarchy was abolished, tabloid newspapers would have no stories and women's magazines wouldn't know what to put on the cover
- ☻ Would you want their descendants in the common gene pool?
- ☻ If the monarchy was abolished, Charles and Di would be free to get divorced (like they're obviously dying to do) and it would be on TV all the time
- ☻ We can all feel positively good-looking by comparison
- ☻ Comedy writers won't have anyone to take the piss out of

22 Things Her Majesty the Queen Will Never Do

- 🔒 Win any beauty contests
- 🔒 Appear as a contestant on *Bob's Your Uncle*
- 🔒 A loud fart in public
- 🔒 Share a bag of chips with you
- 🔒 Send you a signed photograph
- 🔒 Take part in an egg-and-spoon race

- Officially open a car boot sale
- Like Margaret Thatcher
- Tell willie jokes to visiting heads of state
- Write fan letters to Morrisey
- Mud wrestling
- Come round for tea
- Scratch your back for you
- Recommend a good proctologist
- Sunbathe topless in Crete
- Drink from the bottle
- Pole vault for Britain in the Olympics
- Abdicate in favour of Prince Charles
- Abdicate in favour of Richard Stilgoe
- Wear fashionable clothes
- Play practical jokes with plastic dog turds
- Pay tax like the rest of us

---

10 People Princess Diana Has Never Heard of

- ✕ Alan Mullery
- ✕ Mr Sheen
- ✕ Jean-Paul Sartre
- ✕ Barry Sheene
- ✕ Graham Greene
- ✕ Jimmy Cricket
- ✕ Pat Jennings
- ✕ Colonel Sanders
- ✕ Dorothy Perkins
- ✕ You

---

19 Words or Phrases It Would Be Most Unwise to Use in Conversation with Her Majesty the Queen Mother

- ☛ Plop-plops
- ☛ Spermicide jelly

- Jism
- Love blobs
- Douche
- Bum
- Strap on
- Bonk
- Nob hound
- Euthanasia
- Colostomy bag
- Widdle
- Guff
- Crotch cheese
- Winkie
- Detumescent
- Ringpiece
- Penis enlarger
- *Soixante-neuf* (unless addressing Her Majesty in French and referring to something of that denomination)

HRH Prince Charles's 10 Closest Personal Friends

- ◆ HRH Prince Charles
- ◆ Lady Daphne Shrub
- ◆ A bush called Henrietta
- ◆ Rodney Tulip-Bulb
- ◆ The Rt. Hon. Tarquin Oak-Tree
- ◆ The Barclays building in Shoreditch
- ◆ Lord 'Tonky' Hyacinth
- ◆ Terence Twig, the Duke of the Back Garden
- ◆ Earl Cheese Plant of Conservatory Shelf
- ◆ An eight-foot-tall blue Martian called Marmaduke

11 Questions You Shouldn't Ask if You Meet HRH Prince Philip on a Walkabout

☆ What's your favourite kebab, Phil?

☆ How do you reconcile being president of the World Wildlife Fund with killing animals for fun?

☆ Have you got change of 50p for the meter?

☆ Does she 'go'?

☆ Shot any baby animals recently?

☆ Come on, tell me the truth. How did you *really* get all those medals you're wearing?

☆ What's the recipe for kleftiko?

☆ Was it you who just farted?

☆ Can you spare us a quid till payday, mate?

☆ Can you look after my dog while I pop into the supermarket for a sec?

☆ Would you like a salt 'n' vinegar crisp, Your Highness?

13 Games You Can Be Sure the Royals Don't Play at Sandringham

- Hide and Seek
- Strip Poker
- Tag
- Subbuteo
- Postman's Knock
- Kisschase
- Arm wrestling
- Dwarf throwing
- Twister
- Jack the Biscuit
- Super Mario Brothers
- Spin the Bottle
- Darts

'Some Of My Fave Things' by Fergie

☀ Cakes

☀ Buns

☀ Champers

☀ More champers

☀ More cakes and buns

☀ Oh yah, and holidays

☀ And more buns

☀ Anders

☀ Drinking champers on holiday . . . and eating buns

☀ Food fights

☀ Food fights on holiday while drinking champers

☀ Getting all that scrummy money from the Civil List to spend on champers and holidays . . . and buns

☀ And more buns

☀ And more champers

BACK TO SCHOOL

11 Stupid Things They Teach You in Maths That Mean Bugger All When You Leave School

- Logarithms
- Matrices
- Vectors
- Quadratic equations
- Long division
- Topography
- Working out the lowest common denominator
- Binary arithmetic
- Slide rules
- Algebra
- How long it would take 3 men to dig 7 holes working at twice the speed

---

10 Stupid Ways to Cheat at Exams

✗ Use an ex-WWII U-boat periscope to see the answers of the candidate sitting directly in front of you

---

✕ Take all your textbooks into the exam hall, hidden up your jumper

✕ Communicate with a friend outside the exam hall by means of a mobile phone

✕ Write the answers in reverse on your tongue in waterproof ink. When you need to see them, stick your tongue out and look in a hand mirror

✕ Find out who's setting the paper and employ a team of private detectives to follow them around for a while until they dig up some dirt. Then threaten blackmail unless you're supplied with the answers

✕ Make all your textbooks invisible so you can carry them into the exam hall without arousing suspicion

✕ Have your course notes tattooed all down your legs. When you need to check an answer, just remove your trousers or stockings

✕ Develop your latent psychic powers until you're able to read the mind of the class swot sitting 12 desks away

✕ Travel forwards in time and talk to yourself coming out of the exam hall to find out what the questions were

✕ Put down the first answer that comes into your head, then change reality to match your answers

13 Stupid Words or Phrases You Usually Find in Your School Report

- ☛ Tries hard
- ☛ Lazy
- ☛ Easily distracted
- ☛ Could do better
- ☛ Very disruptive
- ☛ Must concentrate
- ☛ Bad influence
- ☛ Heart not in it
- ☛ Inattentive
- ☛ Steady progress
- ☛ Average
- ☛ Sadly lacking
- ☛ Class comedian

11 Stupid Things You'll Always Find at the Very Bottom of Your Child's Schoolbag

- ◆ Somebody else's gym shorts
- ◆ A leaky Biro
- ◆ A boiled sweet with fluff stuck all over it
- ◆ *One* smelly plimsole
- ◆ Sandwich crusts
- ◆ Something black, sticky and totally unidentifiable
- ◆ A crumpled-up school form you were meant to have received four months ago
- ◆ A gaudy pocket calculator with the batteries missing
- ◆ A broken ruler covered in doodles
- ◆ The school tie that went missing last term
- ◆ A joke plastic spider

10 Words You Don't Want to See on Your Child's Report Card

☆ Klepto ☆ Bully

☆ Cretin ☆ Chain smoker

☆ Dense ☆ Failure

☆ Incapable ☆ Despised

☆ Worst ☆ Tasty

7 Stupid Things to Tell Your Children on Their First Day at School

☧ Teachers should always be referred to as 'Mrs Nobface'

☧ Bad ghosts live in the school toilets

☧ If you don't like it, just raise your hand and they'll let you go home

☧ Spitting at other children will help you make lots of new friends

☧ I'll come and collect you after an hour

☧ If you need to go to the toilet, let the teacher know by dropping your trousers

☧ Lessons don't start until 11 a.m., so there's no hurry to get there, is there?

SCIENCE FICTIONS

10 Things That Are Hotter Than You Think

☀ Alpha Centauri

☀ That tip you ignored for the 3.15 at Newmarket

☀ That Pyrex bowl left on the work surface

☀ The Blaupunkt 'Berlin' car radio that you bought from a friend for £40

☀ The plastic cup full of MacDonald's tea that you've just spilled on your lap

☀ The spark plug you've just taken out for checking

☀ The blind date with your sister's friend that you turned down

☀ The police lead on you for buying that £40 car radio

☀ The Bangalore phal chicken curry that you thought sounded interesting

☀ Your bottom, after eating that Bangalore phal chicken curry

1 Fruit That Looks Like a Banana
A banana

10 Things You Can't Do Very Well on the Surface of Mercury

✗ Survive for more than 0.002 seconds

✗ Eat a raspberry Cornetto

✗ Levitate a bowl of fruit, just by looking at it

✗ Travel to Torremolinos on holiday

✗ Play ice hockey

✗ Collect train numbers

✗ Get Pizza Hut to deliver a Spicy Hot One

✗ Watch Arsenal at home

✗ Make a reasonable snowman

✗ Do an honest day's work (a Mercurian day is the equivalent to 59 Earth days)

10 Sneaky Methods of Disposing of Toxic Waste Abroad

☞ Leave it in black plastic bin liners on the French side of the Channel Tunnel at night

☞ Disguise it as models of beefeaters, the Tower of London and policemen's helmets for visiting tourists to take home with them. N.B. A particularly large amount of waste would require a Royal Wedding to stimulate the additional demand for souvenirs. (It is predicted that Prince Edward's marriage would enable

1.4 million tonnes of waste disguised as commemorative plates to be disposed of)

☛ Add it to British wines or sherry for export. (This won't affect their saleability. They all taste like crap, anyway)

☛ Produce an exact replica of the Elgin marbles from decaying plutonium and agree to return them to Greece

☛ Get the Royal Navy invited to make goodwill tours to foreign ports. When it's dark they can throw it off the side of the ships

☛ Before they perform abroad, get the men in the Royal ballet to fill their codpieces with waste. This can then be discreetly jettisoned after the final *pas de deux* when no one's looking

☛ Fill up black plastic sacks with toxic waste and write 'Diplomatic Bag' on them, then dump them abroad somewhere

☛ Make it into condoms and offer them free at airports (the fact that they make the wearer sterile makes them an even better contraceptive)

☛ Jettison it under the guise of coloured smoke by the Red Arrows display team when they're on a world tour

☛ Use toxic waste in the ink used to stamp foreign tourists' passports, and in airmail stickers for envelopes or postcards

9 Smells That Are Quite Unpleasant

◆ A 3-day-old corpse

◆ The underwear of a 3-day-old corpse

◆ The burning exoskeletons of insects heated under a magnifying glass

◆ A Sumo wrestler's loincloth

◆ A jar of sandwich spread that's been left opened on top of a warm radiator for 17 weeks

◆ Farts induced by vegetable biryani

◆ The interior of a Japanese whaling ship

◆ The armpit of the person standing next to you on a crowded train as you're trying to read this book standing up

◆ Brut 33

10 Things Electrical Stores Never Have, But 'Can Order' for You

☆ Atari ST computers

☆ Any other games system you want (or can afford)

☆ Games for the computers which they don't have in stock

☆ Video recorders

☆ Television sets

☆ Hi-fis

☆ Washing machines

☆ The coffee percolator you liked the look of

☆ Anything which works properly when you get it home

☆ A replacement for the faulty electrical goods you're trying to take back

10 Things Which Electrical Stores Do Actually Have in Stock at Any Given Time

✗ Plugs for the electrical goods which they can't sell you because they haven't got any in stock at the moment, but 'can order' for you

✗ A whole wall full of completely useless leads and connectors in plastic bags

✗ Packets and packets of video tapes which would be great except you can't get a video recorder because there's none in stock at the moment

✗ Credit card slips

✗ Goods which a previous customer brought back as faulty, which they're hoping to fob off on to you

✗ Sad men who have worked for 25 years to become assistant manager of the personal stereo department

✗ A wide selection of excuses as to why they can't give you a refund under any circumstances

✗ A complete range of handy ways to fob you off and get you out of the store before other customers notice you're complaining

✗ A full complement of 18-year-old cretins who can't tell you anything about any product on display in the store

* Lots of bullshit about overpriced three-year extended warranties (which are only two years in reality, because the manufacturer's guarantee covers the first year, and which wouldn't be necessary if the equipment was any good in the first place)

10 Plants You Wouldn't Want to Meet in a Dark Alley

* Ellison's bushwacking marigold
* Rhododendrons hell-bent on revenge
* A delinquent foxglove
* The Shrub Gang
* A carnation that thinks it's a triffid
* A lily with a grudge
* A psychopathic dandelion
* A sweet pea desperate for its next fix of crack
* A Venus fly trap with nothing left to lose
* A privet hedge with a semi-automatic weapon

11 Stupid Ways to Try and Prove Your New Scientific Theory

* Toss a coin
* Challenge all sceptics to an arm-wrestling contest
* Ask Sinitta what she thinks
* Say, 'It's right because it is . . .'

- Dissect a Member of Parliament on live television
- Say, 'My horoscope says I'll make a major scientific breakthrough this week . . .'
- Put your hand in a blender and switch it on
- By a combination of martial arts and crochet work
- Put your trousers over your head and chase buses down the high street
- Cite 'indisputable evidence' from articles in the *Sunday Sport*
- With a bunsen burner and a wriggly kitten

10 Unhappy Trees

- ✕ Weeping willows
- ✕ Distraught elms
- ✕ Inconsolable oaks
- ✕ Distressed larches
- ✕ Sobbing figs
- ✕ Manically depressed palms
- ✕ Miserable birch
- ✕ Tormented pines
- ✕ Suicidal bonsais
- ✕ Peeved firs

10 Stupid Facts About the Sun

- It's big
- It's yellow
- It's quite hot
- If you tried to fly there it would take a long time
- It gets in your eyes
- It doesn't really have a hat on

- It's still there, even at night (it's just that we can't see it)
- We all revolve around it
- If it wasn't there, we'd be cold
- Icarus flew too near it (prat)

---

9 Stupid Advantages of Being Abducted by Space Aliens

◆ You might be forced to mate with a creature with six bosoms

◆ You might be forced to mate with a creature with three willies

◆ You'll probably see sights never before seen by human eyes (including the above)

◆ You could sell your story for a big cash sum to the *Sunday Sport*

◆ You could travel at the speed of light and actually get back before you left, so you wouldn't waste any time

◆ You could learn the secret of the Universe, even before breakfast

◆ It's a good excuse for why you're late for work or school

◆ You could get a good job as a consultant on *Close Encounters II*

◆ It makes a change from being abducted by a perv

7 Things That Rutherford Split Before the Atom

☆ His lip

☆ The lip of his arch scientific rival

☆ His head open (after his arch scientific rival smacked him one)

☆ His trousers

☆ His sides (at a stupid joke about relativity)

☆ A banana (inventing a brand-new dessert into the bargain)

☆ His personality

10 Scientists Who Would Have looked Much Better Without Facial Hair

⚷ Louis Pasteur

⚷ Albert Einstein

⚷ Galileo Galilei

⚷ Thomas Alva Edison

⚷ Alfred Nobel

⚷ Max Planck

⚷ Alexander Graham Bell

⚷ Guglielmo Marconi

⚷ John Logie Baird

⚷ Marie Curie

PLAYTIME

16 Stupid Things You're Guaranteed to Find at a British Seaside Resort

- ☀ A beach littered with rusty tin cans, oil, bottles, dog turds, ice lolly sticks and a dead seagull

- ☀ A decrepit 'Esplanade Café' that's always shut

- ☀ Groups of lager louts sitting on the pier railings holding pint glasses and mooning passing families

- ☀ Waving, cooing pensioners with thick coats and expressions, smiling inanely from the promenade train

- ☀ Unpredictable weather (although most days are cold, damp and miserable)

- ☀ No hot water in your B&B after 3.00 p.m. (and precious little before that), a list of restrictions about 90 feet long and a landlady resembling Demis Roussos who'll knock on your door every hour without fail to make sure that you haven't brought any women back to your room

- ☀ The sea maintained at a constant 4°C with raw sewage regularly piped in to

create that familiar grey-brown 'Christ,
I'm not going in there!' look

☺ Prats with metal detectors pacing up and
down the beach like expectant fathers

☺ Fat, ugly people changing their swimming
costumes behind far too skimpy towels

☺ Loudspeakers on the promenade that
constantly blast out a distorted Simon
Bates

☺ Wankers on roller skates and skateboards

☺ Stray dogs doing it behind dilapidated
beach huts

☺ Boring illuminations with one bulb in
three that doesn't work

☺ Cannon and Ball (supported by The
Spinners) perpetually topping the bill at
the Winter Gardens

☺ Hordes of stupid Spanish-looking
students

☺ Discos that still play Frankie Goes to
Hollywood and Earth Wind and Fire, and
which are filled with guys wearing white
socks and sovereign rings who are on the
pull – but getting nowhere and settling
for pushing each other through
plate-glass windows on the esplanade at
2.00 a.m.

7 Stupid Ways to Keep Your Records Clean

▣ Scour them with a Brillo pad soaked in
Vim

▣ Put them in the washing machine on
programme 5

- Screw them to your car roof and drive through a carwash
- Shake them in a sealed container filled with bits of broken glass, razor blades and barbed wire
- Break them over a friend's head
- Soak them in concentrated nitric acid
- Don't ever take them out of their sleeves

11 Other Shapes Footballs Could Be (But Aren't, for Very Good Reasons)

- ✗ Rectangular
- ✗ Sort of blobby with one end sticking up
- ✗ Sort of blobby with the other end sticking up
- ✗ Cubed
- ✗ Pyramid-shaped
- ✗ Mini Metro-shaped
- ✗ Sort of round, but with a star and a twisty bit in the middle
- ✗ Pancake-shaped
- ✗ Trapezoid
- ✗ A shape that exists in six dimensions simultaneously and can only be expressed as a mathematical equation
- ✗ Rugby ball shaped – because then they would be rugby balls

10 Sports Stars Called Steve

- ☛ Steve MacMahon
- ☛ Steve Davies

☛ Steven 'Steve' Hendry

☛ Steve James

☛ Steve Hodge

☛ Steve Cram

☛ Steve Ovett

☛ Steve Heighway

☛ Seve (Steve spelt wrong) Ballesteros

☛ Ian 'Steve' Botham

10 Sports Stars *Not* Called Steve

◆ Sebastian Coe

◆ Fatima Whitbread

◆ Paul 'Gazza' Gascoigne

◆ Terry Butcher

◆ Arnold Palmer

◆ Mike Tyson

◆ Gary Lineker

◆ Alex 'Hurricane' Higgins

◆ Mike Gatting

◆ Bjorn Borg

10 Stupid Things to Do with a Telephone in Your Spare Time

☆ Make obscene phone calls from your office to your home answerphone

☆ Ring up the Tasmanian speaking clock, leave the receiver off the hook and go out for a leisurely walk

☆ Marry it

☆ Make obscene phone calls to the cricket score line

☆ Use it often (if you aren't a multi-millionaire)

☆ Ring up people you don't know and ask for Barry

☆ Ring up people you do know and ask for Barry

☆ Ring up Directory Enquiries and ask for ten numbers you already know

☆ Ring up the AA or RAC and pretend to be in distress in the remotest part of the Lake District

☆ Ring up any 0898 number

12 Genuinely Stupid Sports

ⵟ American football

ⵟ Australian rules football

ⵟ Bobsleighing and tobogganing

ⵟ Curling

ⵟ Cycling

ⵟ Hurling

ⵟ Lacrosse

ⵟ Polo

ⵟ Shinty

ⵟ Trampolining

ⵟ Walking

ⵟ Water polo

10 Stupid People You Don't Want Sitting Near You in the Cinema

☻ Anyone with glazed eyes who makes little gasping sounds under his breath at all the gory moments in the film

☻ Someone who is obviously accompanying a blind friend, because he has to explain what's going on every single moment of the film . . .

- ☺ Someone who eats their popcorn like an asthmatic pig

- ☺ Someone who has seen the film before and insists on telling his friend 'This is a really good bit . . .' or 'Don't look!', every two minutes

- ☺ A child who has just had the largest-sized tub of sugared popcorn and four Westlers and is now looking around for somewhere to be sick

- ☺ An old man who is fast asleep and snoring

- ☺ The local lads' contingent, who act like they're still on the building site whenever any character takes an item of clothing off (even if it's a hat)

- ☺ Someone who thinks the back of your chair (and your collar) is his foot-rest

- ☺ Someone who has dropped a Callard & Bowser down by her feet and is determined to root around and find it, even if it takes her the whole film . . .

- ☺ Someone in a grubby raincoat who you suspect might be frantically rubbing himself under cover of darkness

14 Things You Shouldn't Do in a Public Library

- Hold a shouting contest
- Hold a barbecue, using volumes of the *Encyclopaedia Britannica* as briquettes

- Do your impression of *Krakatoa – East of Java*
- Fly a remote-controlled aircraft
- Pop a succession of crisp packets
- Busk
- Hold an impromptu demonstration of primal scream therapy
- Ask for particular books through a megaphone
- Piss off the librarian by asking for *Fly Fishing* by J.R. Hartley
- Demonstrate your yodelling prowess
- Dress up as a leading Nazi and burn anything that looks fairly intelligent
- Hold a commendably ethnic display of Greek plate-smashing
- Put a sheet over your head, and make ghost noises behind the occult section
- Snigger and point at the people looking at books on how to cope with VD

6 Stupid Things That Always Happen During a Game of Monopoly

- ✗ A fight over who gets to be the Car, the Iron or the Dog (as if it really matters)
- ✗ No one understanding how the mortgages work
- ✗ Arguments over the rules of 'Free Parking'
- ✗ Someone saying something predictable when the card with 'You have won second prize in a beauty contest' is picked up

✗ Someone saying, 'Wouldn't it be great if all this money was real!'

✗ The person who suggested the game in the first place getting bored halfway through

10 Stupid Games or Sports to Play on Your Own

- Kisschase
- American football
- Tug of War
- Spin the Bottle
- Pictionary
- Pass the Parcel
- Hide and Seek
- Postman's Knock
- Cricket
- 4 × 100 metres relay

12 Stupid Names to Call Your Racehorse

- ◆ Lame Boy
- ◆ A Little Slow
- ◆ Lose Your Shirt
- ◆ Dunracing Lad
- ◆ Last Past the Post
- ◆ Stewards' Enquiry
- ◆ Doped Up Git
- ◆ Cat-Meat Certainty
- ◆ Limpy Sam
- ◆ Rank Outsider
- ◆ Knacker's Choice
- ◆ Asthmatic Lass

10 Stupid Things to Use as the Baton in a Relay Race

☆ A small cactus

☆ A scorpion

☆ Anything covered in Superglue

☆ Anything white hot

☆ Anything securely manacled to your wrist

☆ A lit stick of dynamite

☆ An anvil

☆ A baton-shaped piece of margarine

☆ Your willie

☆ Someone else's willie

5 Stupid Places to Go on Holiday if You Want a Serious Sun Tan

🕇 The Falkland Islands

🕇 Alaska

🕇 Greenland

🕇 The South Pole

🕇 Manchester

10 Stupid Things to Do if You Collect Stamps

◎ Cut the perforations off because they look untidy

◎ Staple them into your album

◎ Only collect stamps from countries beginning with 'Y'

◎ After you've catalogued and cross-indexed them, feed them into a paper shredder

◎ Stick your most valuable ones on an envelope and post them to a fictitious address in New Zealand

- ☀ Go into Stanley Gibbons and ask to see the monkeys
- ☀ Colour them all in felt pen and pretend they're Penny Blacks
- ☀ File them in order based on the third letter of the country's name
- ☀ Draw glasses and a moustache on the Queen's portrait
- ☀ Collect coins by mistake

8 Scottish Football Clubs with Stupid Names

- ⚽ Hamilton Academicals
- ⚽ Stenhousemuir
- ⚽ Queen of the South
- ⚽ Partick Thistle
- ⚽ Alloa
- ⚽ Heart of Midlothian
- ⚽ Airdreonians
- ⚽ Meadowbank Thistle

6 Other Football Clubs with Stupid Names

- ✕ Ajax
- ✕ Tottenham Hotspur
- ✕ Dynamo Minsk
- ✕ Zurich Grasshoppers
- ✕ Accrington Stanley
- ✕ Borussia Moenchengladbach

10 Stupid Things You'll Never See at a Bowls Match

- ☛ The crowd on their feet
- ☛ The home supporters singing 'Ere we go, 'ere we go, 'ere we go!'
- ☛ The away supporters singing 'Who's that wanker in the white!'
- ☛ A tackle above the knee
- ☛ A streaker who's under 55
- ☛ Much sign of human life
- ☛ The referee award an indirect free kick
- ☛ The crowd protesting about a handball
- ☛ A nice turn of speed
- ☛ An 'off the ball' incident

11 More Interesting Things to Do Than Watch a Game of Cricket

- ◆ Count the number of cars you see on a 110-mile motorway drive
- ◆ Paint a ceiling in undercoat
- ◆ Pluck every one of the hairs on your arms with tweezers
- ◆ Watch a game of bowls
- ◆ Play solitaire 78 consecutive times
- ◆ Go to night school to learn tax accounting
- ◆ Rewire all the plugs in your house
- ◆ Catalogue all the food in your house according to weight, brand name in alphabetical order and colour of packaging
- ◆ Read everything by Proust

◆ Visit a garden centre
◆ Ring up a financial adviser and ask for advice

Bruce Forsyth's 9 Favourite Chess Moves

☆ P-R3   ☆ R-K1   ☆ P-QKt4
☆ Q-KKt2   ☆ QR-K1   ☆ R-B3
☆ P-K4   ☆ K-K2   ☆ B-KB4

---

10 Stupid Things to Do if You Suddenly Had a Million Pounds

✘ Give it away to the first person you see
✘ Give it away to anyone else
✘ Buy a very valuable painting, set fire to it and then get specially trained 'Poodle Philistines' to dive through the middle of the burning frame
✘ Invest the lot with a broker who contacts you over the phone
✘ Put it all on a horse called Lame-io
✘ Say, 'It won't change my life one little bit!'
✘ Eat it with jam
✘ Hand it in to the police station and claim the £10 reward on offer
✘ Question where it came from
✘ Carry on working

---

12 Stupid Places to Go on Holiday

☀ Beirut
☀ Where you work

☺ Your next-door neighbours' house
☺ Birmingham
☺ The place you went last year and hated
☺ Majorca
☺ Into the cupboard under the stairs
☺ Chernobyl
☺ Anywhere downwind of Chernobyl
☺ Libya
☺ Anywhere else beginning with 'L'
(including Lesotho, Liechtenstein and Laos)
☺ Directly in the path of Hurricane Sharon

10 Top Soccer Players' Favourite Islands

☖ Danny Blanchflower (Madagascar)
☖ Pat Jennings (Sumatra)
☖ Paul 'Gazza' Gascoigne (Switzerland)
☖ Bobby Charlton (Tasmania)
☖ Sir Stanley Matthews (Cuba)
☖ Emlyn Hughes (the Isle of Wight)
☖ John Barnes (Kos)
☖ Billy Bremner (Baffin Island)
☖ Kenny Dalglish (Tobago)
☖ Bobby Moore (Corsica)

9 Stupid Things Your Holiday Brochure Says (and What They Really Mean)

✗ *Well-established resort* . . . This resort
used to be quite nice . . . until the British
discovered it. Now it's a cross between

Hades, Saturday night in Ilford and a bucket of poo

✗ *Becomes busy between May and September* . . . Most of the town is unsafe between May and September (unless you support Millwall)

✗ *A popular destination for the young and with-it* . . . Great if you like arseholes, otherwise avoid like the plague

✗ *A very popular, traditional budget-priced hotel* . . . This two-star hotel is utter shite, but we get very preferential terms for using it. Staff are indifferent, hygiene is Turkish in its awfulness and if you stand outside the main entrance, some drunken British thug will invariably piss off the balcony on to your head

✗ *Cosmopolitan clientele* . . . No chance whatsoever of getting a sunbed, because the place is full of Germans

✗ *Convenient location* . . . Miles from the beach (but with the overpowering smell of untreated sewage, cheap suntan lotion and BO wafting off it, that's a blessing as far as we are concerned)

✗ *Now under new management* . . . The old manager is still in a coma, following last year's 'Welcome British Holidaymakers' sangria party which got tragically out of hand

✗ *British food served* . . . Juan the chef has been warned that, unless he wants his fingers broken for a third time, there's going to be no more foreign muck served up

✗ *Always plenty to do . . .* Drinking, fighting the Krauts and Dagos, more drinking, building obscene sandcastles on the beach, more bevvies, some things that will make *News at Ten* back home, dodging the Spanish National Guard, more bevvies, vomit in town square, vomit in 'El Londoner' disco, vomit off the balcony, get food poisoning and have to spend the rest of the holiday in bed

10 Stupid Occupations to Put on Your Passport

- ☛ Ocelot masturbator
- ☛ Criminal mastermind
- ☛ Drugs baron
- ☛ Professional sperm donor
- ☛ Locomotive juggler
- ☛ Self-employed wiggly dancer
- ☛ Catheter fitter to the crowned heads of Europe
- ☛ Napalm taster
- ☛ Unicellular life form
- ☛ Civil servant

ON THE ROAD

13 Things People Think to Themselves on a Crowded Train

◆ Turn that fucking Walkman off or I'll punch it down your throat

◆ Ha, ha! I've got a seat and you haven't

◆ I wonder what he/she's like in bed

◆ Prat

◆ If she would just move her leg a bit I could see right up her skirt

◆ Phworrrr! Who farted?

◆ I wish he'd stop sniffing and blow his nose

◆ I wish this erection would go down

◆ Why do the horny girls always get into the other carriages?

◆ I hope that loony doesn't come anywhere near me

◆ Don't fancy yours, mate

◆ I'm going to be late

◆ I'm going to be very late

10 Things It's Not Advisable to Do with Your Car

☆ Drive it everywhere at 60 m.p.h. in reverse

☆ Report it stolen, collect the insurance money and then drive it back and forth outside a police station with the horn blaring

☆ Pour concentrated hydrofluoric acid all over the paintwork

☆ Leave it outside a scrapyard with a big sign on the roof saying 'Not Wanted'

☆ Submerge it in a nearby canal

☆ Force the lock, smash the window and rip out the stereo

☆ Attempt to leap over 14 double-decker buses parked side by side on live TV

☆ Drive the wrong way around the M25 about 4.30 on a Friday afternoon

☆ Trade it in for a P-reg Austin Allegro

☆ Lend it free of charge to a minicab company

12 Stupid Things You Always See Stuffed Down Between a Van's Dashboard and Windscreen

☧ One loudspeaker with two wires trailing from it

☧ A tatty *A–Z* with the last 10 pages missing

☧ Packet of Embassy No.1s

☧ Assorted scrunched-up pieces of paper,

business cards, parking tickets and petrol
receipts
- A screwdriver with a yellow handle and a
  piece of ½" copper pipe
- A transistor radio
- Yesterday's *Sporting Life*
- Out-of-date tax disc
- Old Biros that don't work
- Half-empty MacDonald's milkshake
  carton
- Three cassettes without cases
- A pair of sunglasses with one of the arms
  missing

11 of the Worst Drivers to Get Stuck Behind

- An old lady in a Morris Minor
- An old man in a Morris Minor
- An old couple in a Morris Minor
- Anyone else in a Morris Minor
- Anyone towing a caravan
- Anyone wearing a hat (especially if
  they're in a Morris Minor)
- Anyone in a hearse, milkfloat, tractor or
  steamroller
- Anyone from abroad
- Anyone who has no prior knowledge of
  how to control a motor vehicle
- Anyone who's stationary
- Anyone who's suddenly decided to
  reverse all the way home

10 Stupid Things to Lose on a Train

- Your fight against terminal syphilis
- All hope of ever finding any survivors
- Your way
- Your mind
- Your struggle against an imperialist society
- A case containing all your ticket-forging equipment with your name and address inside it
- Your grip on reality
- All sense of direction
- Your independence
- Face

7 Motoring Awards Won by the Lada Riva

- ✕ 1987: Outright Winner 'Car I'd Least Like to Own'
- ✕ 1988: Outright Winner 'Car I'd Still Least Like to Own'
- ✕ 1988: 'Low Performance Car of the Year'
- ✕ 1989: Overall Winner of Germany's *Autoschiesen* trophy
- ✕ 1990: Outright Champion 'Car I'd Least Like to Be Seen Driving'
- ✕ 1990: Auto Manufacturers' Special 'Shame on the Industry' Award
- ✕ 1990: Industrie de Méchanique Français *'Voiture Merde de l'Année'*

15 Stupid Things You See on the Motorway

- ☛ Cretins driving cars
- ☛ Cretins driving vans
- ☛ Cretins driving lorries
- ☛ Miles of seemingly pointless traffic cones
- ☛ Disregard for safe braking distances
- ☛ Squashed wildlife
- ☛ A Porsche or BMW with a blonde in the passenger seat, going past you at 130 m.p.h.
- ☛ Spectacular errors of judgement
- ☛ Somewhat interesting lane discipline
- ☛ People flashing their lights at each other, making frantic V-signs and mouthing obscenities
- ☛ Speeds that would make Emerson Fittipaldi shit himself
- ☛ People taking the wrong exit, realising their mistake at the last moment and swerving back straight in front of you
- ☛ People waiting for the RAC
- ☛ The lorry in front of you shedding half its load directly in your path
- ☛ Loads of hitchhikers you don't fancy

10 Things You Never See on a Hell's Angel's Harley Davidson

- ◆ A bell with a picture of Mickey Mouse on it
- ◆ Stabilisers

◆ Bubblegum cards in the spokes

◆ Stickers from a packet of breakfast cereal

◆ A horn that plays 'La Cucaracha'

◆ L plates

◆ A bottle attached to the handlebars containing orange squash

◆ Anything pink

◆ A transfer that says 'BMX Bandit'

◆ Angela Rippon

11 Things You Never See in a Minicab

☆ A copy of the Highway Code

☆ A book entitled *Improving the Harmony of a Multiracial Society*

☆ Any other book

☆ Empty ashtrays

☆ The speedometer needle under 70 m.p.h.

☆ A radio that you can actually hear from the back seat

☆ An interior that looks like it's been vacuumed at least once since new

☆ A horn that's virtually unused

☆ A fare system that doesn't appear to be made up on the spot

☆ Receipts, when you actually need them

☆ The Queen

9 Things You Never Hear Used-Car Salesmen Say

✗ Name your price

✗ It was previously owned by a well-known hire company

✗ If you look under the carpet you can see that it's been completely resprayed

✗ I think it's actually two different cars, both insurance write-offs, welded together

✗ I wouldn't trust the milometer if I were you, sir. It's probably been round the clock at least three times

✗ The previous owner died because the brakes failed for no apparent reason

✗ That little squeak? I'd say it was something major

✗ And we'll guarantee it against any defect for 5 years or 100,000 miles

✗ They don't all do that, sir

11 Stupid Things to Do During Your Driving Test

☉ Blindfold yourself and drive using your psychic powers

☉ Slam the examiner's hand in the door repeatedly until he either passes you or calls the police

☉ Operate the gearstick with your mouth

☉ Perform an emergency stop at a time and place of your own choosing

- When you're asked to read a numberplate at 25 feet, refuse
- Pretend to be pissed
- Actually be pissed
- Act as though you've only got the use of one leg
- Run a tube from the exhaust pipe into the interior of your car for the hell of it
- Say 'Man opening umbrella' if you're asked to identify the 'Roadworks' sign
- Do the whole thing perfectly – only in reverse

10 Parts of a Car That Sound a Bit Rude

- Wankel engine
- Half shaft
- Piston
- Big end
- Crank
- Push rod
- Sump
- Thrust bearing
- Dipstick
- Ball joint

10 Stupid Ways to Identify a Ferrari Owner

- ✗ He's got a really small willie
- ✗ His favourite colour is red
- ✗ You wouldn't trust him further than you could spit
- ✗ He thinks Porsches are dull
- ✗ He's embarrassed when a man asks what car he drives
- ✗ He's only too willing to admit what car he drives when a woman asks

✗ He tries to act like he's 10 years younger
✗ He tries to act like he's 30 lbs lighter
✗ He says things like 'Yeah! Groovy!'
✗ He's got a Ferrari

10 People It's Not Really Advisable to Pick up as Hitchhikers

☞ Anyone who's easily influenced and who's seen *The Hitcher* with Rutger Hauer 27 times

☞ Anyone carrying a sack of money and a sawn-off shotgun

☞ Anyone wearing a ski-mask, especially if it's the middle of summer

☞ Anyone whose best friend was murdered by a driver giving them a lift and who's out to get revenge

☞ Anyone who wants to go in completely the opposite direction

☞ Anyone holding a sign that says 'John o'Groats' (unless you happen to be in Thurso at the time)

☞ Anyone holding a sign that says 'Hell and back'

☞ Anyone who looks 12 years old holding a sign that says 'All the way, big boy'

☞ Anyone who looks like a phantom

☞ Anyone with matted clothing who obviously suffers from severe travel sickness

10 Stupid Ways to Pass the Time on the Train to Work

◆ Try and work out if the girl standing in the corner is wearing culottes or a skirt

◆ See how long you can hold your breath between stations

◆ Try and think of alternative (and better) headlines for all the advertisements in the carriage. It shouldn't be too difficult

◆ Have a giggle by reading all the advertisements in the carriage but replacing any word beginning with 'A' by the word 'Twat' and any word beginning with 'B' by the word 'Bum'. (E.g. 'British Airways. The world's favourite airline' becomes 'Bum Twat. The world's favourite Twat')

◆ Try and estimate (to the nearest 15 minutes) how late you're going to be

◆ Imagine who you'd eat first if the train got stuck in a tunnel with the doors jammed, for more than 72 hours

◆ Do the 73 times table in your head (if this comes easily, how about recalling all the prime numbers between 417 and 1043?)

◆ Pretend to have a convincing twitch

◆ Try to outstare the person opposite you until they either get up and leave, hit you in the head or say something suggestive

◆ Using your feet, drum through every one of the tracks on Phil Collins' latest solo album

WAGE SLAVES

11 Stupid Things for Yes-Men to Say

☆ I don't think so

☆ Perhaps

☆ Never!

☆ No

☆ No siree

☆ Maybe

☆ Negative

☆ I'm not sure

☆ Let me think about it

☆ Definitely not

☆ Not for a million pounds

---

12 Stupid Jobs Guaranteed Not to Impress Your Girlfriend's Parents

☧ Professional drag artiste

☧ Chief vivisectionist

☧ Serial killer

☧ Staff training officer at Woolworth's

- Mortician
- Anarchist
- Commander of a Japanese whaling fleet
- The man who cuts the electricity off in old people's houses
- Sperm donor
- Gigolo
- The man who centrifuges urine down at the local hospital
- Inventor of the C5

8 Jobs Without Long-Term Prospects

- Kamikaze pilot
- The man who says 'Mind the gap' at Victoria tube station
- The 48th person in line to the throne
- The man who pulls the switch for the electric chair
- The leader of the SDP
- The man who ends the Grand Prix by waving a chequered flag
- The man who says '5, 4, 3, 2, 1 . . . We have liftoff' at the start of the space shuttle launch
- The talking clock

10 Stupid and Heartless Rumours to Spread at Someone's Leaving Party

- She was caught with her hands in the till
- She was caught with her hands in the sales director's underpants

- 🔲 She was caught with her hands in her own underpants
- 🔲 She wants to move on to a firm where her reputation won't stand in the way of her promotion prospects
- 🔲 The boss found out she was moonlighting as a strippogram girl in her tea break
- 🔲 She's pregnant
- 🔲 Cosmetic surgery on that scale can take months
- 🔲 Some people in high places took offence at all those lovebites . . .
- 🔲 She's going to live on a commune with some very strange American women
- 🔲 She thinks she's too good for us

4 Cruel and Stupid Things to Do at Someone's Leaving Party

- ✗ Spike the office coffee machine with laxative before the party, so that no one turns up and she thinks everyone hates her

- ✗ Wrap up the coffee machine and present it to her, saying, 'We won't need this to keep us awake now you're going'

- ✗ Say, 'I tried to organise a collection for you but, strangely, no one seemed to have any money on them all week, so I made you this necklace out of paperclips and a hat out of A3 cartridge. . . . I hope you'll think of us whenever you wear them'

✕ Don't bother to get the card signed – just staple the internal office telephone list to it

10 Things Which Will Not Help Your Career Prospects

☛ Chronic BO
☛ Slaughtering your company's best customers in a Satanic death ritual
☛ Headbutting the chairman
☛ Dressing up as a saucy French maid at the annual sales conference
☛ Appearing on the telly to complain about your company's lousy products
☛ Using kung fu on junior staff
☛ Being caught taking the personnel manager's wife over the office photocopier
☛ Crapping in the fax machine and then repeatedly trying to fax it through to your Glasgow office until forcibly restrained by Security
☛ Pretending that you suddenly speak only Flemish
☛ Getting a degree

7 Ideal Jobs for the Deaf

◆ Customer complaints manager at British Rail
◆ The person who has to mix all the Dannii Minogue singles

- ◆ Derek Hatton's biographer
- ◆ Loyd Grossman's housekeeper
- ◆ Sensitive doctors, specialising in treating flatulence without sniggering...
- ◆ Introducing the British Top 40 on the radio
- ◆ Directory enquiries

10 Things Local Councillors Are Good for

- ☆ Fertiliser
- ☆ Cocking things up
- ☆ Keeping Freemasonry up to strength
- ☆ Giving your town a totally baffling one-way system
- ☆ Slipping an envelope full of used tenners to
- ☆ Going on jollies to your twin town twice a year at your expense
- ☆ Increasing your poll tax every year to help pay for their incompetence
- ☆ Paying you no heed whatsoever
- ☆ Going on holidays to the Caribbean courtesy of local property speculators
- ☆ Sending the bailiffs around to your house

1 Other Thing That Local Councillors Are Good for
☧ Nothing

What Estate Agents Say – and What They Really Mean

- *Internal inspection highly recommended* (Looks a state from the outside)
- *Bijou* (No room to swing a cat)
- *Compact* (No room to swing a mouse)
- *Wildlife garden* (Never been weeded)
- *Lovingly restored* (Chintzy, with purple walls)
- *Needs some attention* (Needs some underpinning)
- *Quiet location* (Miles from the shops)
- *Terraced* (Unbearable noise levels)
- *Modern* (Shoddily built with no damp course)
- *Easily maintained garden* (Tiny)
- *Townhouse* (Situated near busy dual carriageway)
- *Georgian/mock Tudor* (Overpriced)
- *Off-street parking* (There's an NCP ½ mile down the road)
- *Convenient for school* (Next door to a borstal-type institution)
- *Convenient for shops* (Located directly over the Akropolis Kebab Shop)
- *Spacious* (If you're used to living in a coal bunker, for example)
- *All-electric* (Expensive to run)
- *Open-plan front garden* (Tradesmen use lawn as short cut)

- ☀ *No chain* (Someone has died here recently)
- ☀ *Highly sought-after location* (Lots of burglaries in the road)
- ☀ *Converted* (Half a house for three quarters of the price)
- ☀ *Studio* (Bedsit)
- ☀ *Outbuildings* (Derelict shed and outside WC)
- ☀ *Prestigious new development* (Desperate to sell)
- ☀ *Many original features* (Dodgy plumbing, oil lamps and condensation)
- ☀ *Unusual* (Designer was a looney)
- ☀ *Charming* (Old)
- ☀ *Period* (Needs £15,000 worth of repairs)
- ☀ *Family home* (Boring and mass produced)
- ☀ *Reduced for quick sale* (Grossly overpriced in the first place)
- ☀ *Ideal for first-time buyers* (Small and full of faults which you're too inexperienced to spot)
- ☀ *Must be viewed* (Only two people have looked at it)
- ☀ *Reduced* (No one has looked at it)
- ☀ *Olde worlde* (Cesspit in garden)

10 Names *Not* to Call Your New Company

- ▚ The Winkie Fly-By-Night Rip-Off Merchants

- The James Dean School of Motoring
- The Smeggy Bogie Wee-Wee Catering Company
- Fuck the Taxman Ltd
- VAT Swindlers Inc
- The Colwyn Bay Titanic Lusitania Mary Rose Pleasure Cruisers
- The Unlucky Financial Consultants Under a Gypsy Curse PLC
- The Don't Pay Their Bills Co Ltd
- Swizzes-R-Us
- The Hitler, Goebbels and Mosley Memorial Salt Beef Company

11 Jobs It's Unrealistic to Expect You'll Ever Have

- ✕ US Navy 'Top Gun' fighter pilot
- ✕ Prime minister of Belgium
- ✕ Product tester for Ind Coope
- ✕ Spiritual leader of the Cheyenne Indians
- ✕ Mel Gibson's double
- ✕ Captain of the Starship *Enterprise*
- ✕ Special adviser to the United Nations on confectionery matters
- ✕ A hitman for Millets
- ✕ Kim Basinger's body slave
- ✕ Melvyn Bragg's martial arts instructor
- ✕ Anything that's much good, well paid or satisfying

10 Annoying Things About Stupid Photocopiers

☛ They switch to A3 as soon as you start to copy something that's A4

☛ They switch to A4 as soon as you start to copy something that's A3

☛ They're never switched on when you get to work especially early

☛ They always jam just when you're photocopying something personal, like the manuscript for a book

☛ The 'low paper' warning light comes on for no apparent reason

☛ 1 page out of every 20 that you put through on automatic feed does not get copied

☛ Whenever the paper runs out, the nearest ream is two floors away

☛ A queue immediately forms just as soon as you think the coast is clear and you can copy your CV

☛ There's always one staple you forget to remove that jams up the automatic feed

☛ The repair man always chats up the one secretary you're trying to get off with

10 Things You Never Hear from Your Dentist

◆ Yes, you *are* brushing your teeth correctly

◆ Of course it will hurt

◆ Forget it, it's free

◆ Close wide

◆ Golf? I can't stand the game

◆ You can owe it to me

◆ Your teeth are absolutely perfect and there's nothing that needs doing, not even descaling

◆ Of course I don't fancy my dental nurse. I'm a happily married man

◆ Don't bother going private – I can do this treatment on the NHS

◆ Why did I go into dentistry? Well, to help the never-ending struggle against decay and fight for better teeth for all

---

1 Stupid Thing That People Who Work in Advertising Should Never Tell Clients

☆ The truth

---

16 People Not to Get on the Wrong Side of

✗ Freemasons

✗ Book reviewers

✗ Book reviewers who are also Freemasons

✗ Newspaper publishers

✗ Anyone bigger than you

✗ Anyone smaller than you, but who knows the Krays

✗ Anyone remotely connected with the Mafia

✗ Mike Tyson

✗ Islamic fundamentalists

✗ Your bank manager

    ✗ Your boss
   ✗ Anyone with PMT
    ✗ Your hairdresser
   ✗ Your plastic surgeon
   ✗ The Inland Revenue
     ✗ Mossad

10 Stupid Names for a Pub

☀ The Stale Pasty and Listeria
☀ The Pig and Breathalyser
☀ The Flat Beer and Firkin
☀ The Away Supporters' Arms
☀ The Gnat's Piss Inn
☀ The Three Empty Barrels
☀ The Jolly Short Measurer
☀ The Contagious Barman
☀ The Lager Lout and Brawl
☀ The Milk Bar

10 Stupid Signs to Put in Your Shop Window if You're Having a Sale

▣ We're not having a sale!
▣ Closed!
▣ Everything mustn't go!
▣ !ELAS
▣ Only crap left
▣ Everything twice the price!
▣ First few days!

🛍 Everything must stay!
🛍 Massive increases!
🛍 Armadillo!

10 Stupid Questions to Ask at Your Job Interview

✗ Who's that old bag in the photo on your desk?

✗ How much money do you keep in the safe overnight?

✗ When was the last time you had a bath?

✗ My mate works here. He says it's money for old rope. Is that right?

✗ How much sick leave can I take before questions get asked?

✗ What is the capital of Mozambique?

✗ Do you 'go'?

✗ Is that a wig?

✗ Is that all you're paying, you tight-fisted git?

✗ Do you mind if I roll a joint? I can't get through the day without one

3 Particularly Stupid Ways to Try and Make Friends at the Office

☛ Hold a 'Who is the Real Father of the Receptionist's Baby' Sweepstake:

Jim the Janitor	70–1
Dean in Despatch	3–2
Mr Jones, Company Accountant	500–1

Richard in Sales   7–1

Bob in Sales   6–2

Larry in Sales   5–1

Jonathan in Sales   2–1

One of the decorators   5–2

The man who services the
photocopier   11–2

Mr Papadopolous from the
sandwich bar   20–1

Her driving instructor   8–1

Her boyfriend, Les   9000–1

☛ Write a crossword for the in-house
magazine

Across
1. Sleeps with customers to obtain orders (5,5)
4. Jon in Accounts's big secret. He's – (3)
7. The typing pool reckon his is the smallest (4,6)
9. Lisa's just a girl who can't say – (2)
11. Liz is only going out with him for his money
(3,5)
12. Cross-dresser in Marketing (first name) (4)
15. Rachel lost this at 12 (9)
16. Who we hide from when we go down the pub
(6,6)
18. Tnuc – anagram of what Brian calls the MD
(4)
20. What Rick Harris has apparently been one
short of since Korea (4)
22. Smells (surname) (9)
23. Michelle in Bought Ledger's favourite sex act
(initials) (2)
25. Is for the chop, but doesn't know it yet (first
name) (5)

28. The fattest girl in the company (5,7)

30. *Says* she's a natural blonde (4,5)

31. Must spend all of £25 on his suits (4,7)

Down

1. Didn't get kissed under the mistletoe at the last office party (because he's repulsive) (3,8)

2. Receives backhanders from the photocopier suppliers (surname) (8)

3. Boyfriend just left her for her younger sister (first name) (5)

4. Gave Katy in Personnel gonorrhoea (6,4)

5. Has vaginal warts according to 1 across (4,7)

6. Caught masturbating in stock room and claimed to have knocked over the Tipp-Ex (3,8)

8. Has permanent PMT, according to the typing pool (surname) (6)

10. Naffest haircut in western world (surname) (9)

11. Secretly phones her boyfriend in Australia at 11 every day (surname) (8)

12. Failed miserably to get off with 23 across on office outing (4,7)

13. Has a crush on the MD (surname) (3)

14. What Phil and Shelley do on overtime (slang) (4)

15. Our nickname for Julie (slang) (4)

17. He's using Valerie – and she's too young to see it (6,4)

19. So desperate, she's turned to a dating agency (surname) (7)

21. Says the MD's secretary looks like an iguana (4,5)

22. Urinated in the supervisor's coffee mug for a dare (first name) (4)

24. Petty cash forms are a major work of fiction (surname) (6)

25. Two-timing Paul in Goods-Inwards with 4 down (first name) (2)

26. Hasn't lost it yet – and he's 28 (first name) (3)

27. Feeds half his work into the shredder when no one's looking (surname) (3)

29. Makes such loud noises in the Ladies that we can hear her in reception (first name) (3)

☛ Get hold of someone's ledger – and change all the 5s to 8s

---

12 Phrases You Don't Want to Overhear When Your Doctor's Talking About You

◆ 2 months maximum

◆ 2 inches minimum

◆ I'd say 50–50, if that

◆ Who knows?

◆ Who cares?

◆ Below the knee

◆ Below the neck

◆ Big strap to bite on

◆ Impotent for the rest of his life

◆ Next of kin

◆ Isolation ward, and hurry!

◆ Call the circus

---

10 Things You Never Hear Politicians Say on TV

☆ 'Yes'

☆ 'No'

☆ 'I'm having a torrid affair with a prostitute'

- ☆ 'I'm having a torrid affair with the Prime Minister'
- ☆ 'What we really need is a fascist dictator'
- ☆ 'I'm on the payroll of three major arms manufacturers'
- ☆ 'The right honourable member for the opposition has a bloody good point!'
- ☆ 'I'm appearing in *Cinderella* at the Scarborough Roxy'
- ☆ Anything that can't be said in half the words
- ☆ Anything you agree with

---

5 Stupid Things Mark Wishes He Could Do at Work

- Have a chair that didn't wobble from side to side every time he moved his bottom
- Tell clients to fuck off without fear of instant dismissal
- See Debbie Taylor in a skimpy bikini
- Get home in under an hour
- Take home an extra £5000

---

10 Jobs You Don't Often See Advertised Down at Your Local Careers Office

- Nazi hunter
- Speaker of the House of Commons
- Atomic physicist
- Double agent
- Ranch hand

- Space shuttle pilot
- Human guinea pig
- Pioneering brain surgeon
- Queen
- Film director

11 Stupid Jobs Guaranteed Not to Impress Your Boyfriend's Parents

- Dominatrix
- Surrogate mother
- Vibrator tester
- Traffic warden
- Gangster's moll
- Sexologist
- Masseuse
- Trollop
- Saucy kissogram
- Professional mistress
- Female impersonator

WHAT A WONDERFUL WORLD

8 Rivals to the Infamous 'Bermuda Triangle'

- ✗ The Bahamas Oblong
- ✗ The Montserrat Trapezium
- ✗ The St Lucia Circle
- ✗ The Jamaica Ellipse
- ✗ The Barbados Rhomboid
- ✗ The Trinidad and Tobago Parallelogram
- ✗ The Antigua Hexagon
- ✗ The Kennington Oval

12 Places in Great Britain Named After Creatures

- Catford
- Isle of Dogs
- Lizard
- Cowley
- Oxford
- Leighton Buzzard
- Swanage
- Cowes
- Wales
- Shrewsbury
- Wolverhampton
- Manchester

5 Countries with Flags That Are Quite Difficult to Draw

◆ Bhutan (rectangle divided into red and orange triangles with some kind of ornate Chinese-looking serpent in the middle)

◆ Dominica (something that looks like a green parrot in a red circle, surrounded by ten green stars. The circle is in the centre of a yellow, black and white striped cross with green bits in the corners)

◆ South Korea (a ball made up of interlocking 'squiggly' red and blue shapes on a white background. Around the ball are four different patterns that look as though they're from a 'Spot the Odd One Out' test)

◆ Papua, New Guinea (rectangle divided into two triangles. The black one contains six white stars, four big ones and two smaller ones, while the red triangle contains some sort of tropical bird with a long tail)

◆ Brazil (yellow diamond shape set in a green rectangle. In the yellow diamond is a sort of blue globe with a band running where the equator should be. There's some writing or symbols in this band but the picture in the reference book we're using is too small to make it out properly)

11 Stupid Things to Tell Foreign Tourists in London

☆ It's considered good luck to stroke a guardsman's busby

☆ The nearest tube station to Buckingham Palace is Ongar

☆ You can fish for salmon off Westminster Bridge

☆ Horatio Nelson was the founder of London and had four pet lions

☆ It is almost obligatory to haggle with taxi drivers over the fare

☆ The traditional term of address for a London policeman is 'wanker'

☆ A yellow line indicates free parking for one hour (a double yellow line indicates two hours)

☆ There is no speed limit along the Embankment between 11 p.m. and 5 a.m.

☆ All Commonwealth citizens are entitled to one private audience with the Queen each year. Simply present yourself at the main gate in formal dress

☆ The Old Kent Road is famed for its gay
   pubs

☆ In summer, nude sunbathing is permitted
   in only one of the Royal Parks; this is St
   James's Park, off the Mall

---

91 *Real* Places in America Which Sound Stupid

✗ Arab, Alabama

✗ Avon, Alabama

✗ Bibb, Alabama

✗ Coy, Alabama

✗ Lower Peach
   Tree, Alabama

✗ Moody, Alabama

✗ Opp, Alabama

✗ Pisgah, Alabama

✗ Prattville,
   Alabama

✗ Snead, Alabama

✗ Wetumpka,
   Alabama

✗ King Salmon,
   Alaska

✗ Bagdad, Arizona

✗ Chloride, Arizona

✗ El Mirage,
   Arizona

✗ Tuba City,
   Arizona

✗ Winkelman,
   Arizona

✗ Biggers, Arkansas

✗ Flippin, Arkansas

✗ Grubbs, Arkansas

✗ Tontitown,
   Arkansas

✗ Weiner, Arkansas

✗ Loleta, California

✗ Lompoc,
   California

✗ Pismo Beach,
   California

✗ Truckee,
   California

✗ Weimar,
   California

- Dinosaur, Colorado
- Hygiene, Colorado
- Security, Colorado
- Swink, Colorado
- Orange, Connecticut
- The Norman G. Wilder Wildlife Area, Delaware
- Cocoa, Florida
- Homosassa, Florida
- Ponce de Leon, Florida
- Bibb City, Georgia
- Chickamunga, Georgia
- Experiment, Georgia
- Montezuma, Georgia
- Social Circle, Georgia
- Zebulon, Georgia
- Fruitland, Idaho
- Idaho, Idaho
- Energy, Illinois
- Kankakee, Illinois
- Odin, Illinois
- Vermillion, Illinois
- Munster, Indiana
- Poseyville, Indiana
- Santa Claus, Indiana
- Tippecanoe, Indiana
- Early, Iowa
- Lost Nation, Iowa
- Mechanicsville, Iowa
- Titonka, Iowa
- Pratt, Iowa
- Tonganoxie, Iowa
- Big Clifty, Kentucky
- Cranks, Kentucky
- Flat Lick, Kentucky
- Raccoon, Kentucky
- Zebulon, Kentucky
- Truth or Consequences, New Mexico

- ✗ Grosse Tete, Louisiana
- ✗ West Peru, Maine
- ✗ Princess Anne, Maryland
- ✗ Whiskey Bottom, Maryland
- ✗ Dorothy Pond, Massachusetts
- ✗ North Uxbridge, Massachusetts
- ✗ West Acton, Massachusetts
- ✗ Ovid, Michigan
- ✗ Vulcan, Michigan
- ✗ Knob Noster, Missouri
- ✗ Pilot Knob, Missouri
- ✗ Flathead, Montana
- ✗ Cheesequake, New Jersey
- ✗ Dickey, North Dakota
- ✗ Gackle, North Dakota
- ✗ Dry Run, Ohio
- ✗ Mingo Junction, Ohio
- ✗ Cement, Oklahoma
- ✗ Talent, Oregon
- ✗ Berks, Pennsylvania
- ✗ Wounded Knee, South Dakota
- ✗ Soddy-Daisy, Tennessee
- ✗ Deaf Smith, Texas
- ✗ Lolita, Texas
- ✗ Bland, Virginia
- ✗ Isle of Wight, Virginia
- ✗ Belgium, Wisconsin

The 2 Things That Are Fundamentally Wrong with Belgium as a Nation

- ☀ It exists
- ☀ Belgians live there

10 Unsuitable Names for Brutal Fascist Dictators

- Fred
- Chuck
- Elvis
- Franky
- Bert
- Bobby
- Benny
- Nobby
- Tim
- Ian

36 *Real* Places in America Which Sound Rude

- ✕ Boggstown, Indiana
- ✕ Hornell, New York
- ✕ Beaver, Kentucky
- ✕ Trussville, Alabama
- ✕ Prattville, Alabama
- ✕ Fruitdale, Alabama
- ✕ Bald Knob, Arkansas
- ✕ Bent, Colorado
- ✕ Grays Knob, Kentucky
- ✕ French Lick, Indiana
- ✕ Floyds Knob, Indiana
- ✕ Lolita, Texas
- ✕ Rogersville, Kentucky
- ✕ Flushing, Ohio
- ✕ Sodus, New York
- ✕ Cockeysville, Maryland
- ✕ Colon, Michigan
- ✕ Big Beaver, Pennsylvania

✘ Climax, Michigan

✘ Licking, Missouri

✘ Big Horn, Wyoming

✘ Pollock, Idaho

✘ Coxsackie, New York

✘ The Little Big Horn, Montana

✘ Butte Valley, Nevada

✘ Hooker, Nebraska

✘ Biggers, Missouri

✘ Cokato, Minnesota

✘ Butte City, California

✘ Crested Butte, Colorado

✘ Willimantic, Connecticut

✘ Tampa, Florida

✘ Peoria, Illinois

✘ Effingham, Illinois

✘ Intercourse, Pennsylvania

✘ Wanker's Corner, Oregon

The Top 10 Causes of Death in Belgium

☛ Boredom

☛ Falling off bicycles

☛ The stress of playing Belgian Trivial Pursuit

☛ Shock induced by something interesting suddenly happening

☛ Suicide after being refused an emigration permit

☛ Accidental exposure to a fairly interesting paperback or magazine

☛ Falling into a coma and having Belgian doctors try to revive you by playing you a personal message from Belgium's top pop star

☛ Overdosing on chocolate truffles

☛ Exhaustion brought about by trying to find something interesting to do on Saturday night

☛ Simply losing the will to live

7 Things the Japanese Kill Which They Shouldn't

◆ Whales

◆ Dolphins

◆ Porpoises

◆ Anything else that is endangered

◆ The Western electronics industry

◆ Any concept of fair trading practices

◆ POWs

11 Things It Must Be Very Easy to Sell to the Japanese

☆ Elevator shoes

☆ Plastic yellow dick extensions

☆ Penis enlargers

☆ Dental braces

☆ Harpoons

☆ Blue whale ashtrays

☆ Anything else that was once an integral part of an endangered species

☆ A self-help book entitled *How to Work Harder and Die Younger*

☆ A matching set of dolphin-skin luggage

☆ Anything their company says they should have

☆ The idea that they can totally ignore what the rest of the world thinks

11 Things That the Belgians Are Not Very Good at

✗ Throwing wild parties

✗ Letting their hair down

✗ Pop music

✗ Holding their drink

✗ Telling dirty jokes

✗ Starting trends

✗ Vandalism

✗ Football hooliganism

✗ Revolutionising the way we live

✗ Making major motion pictures

✗ Celebrating (but, to be fair, they have never had anything to celebrate)

11 Things That the Belgians *Are* Good at

☻ Staying at home with a good book

☻ Listening to the wireless

☻ Keeping the garden and allotment in good order

☻ Making luxurious confectionery

☺ Knitting and fretwork

☺ Wearing sensible sweaters and comfortable shoes

☺ Knowing when they need a haircut

☺ Remembering people's birthdays

☺ Keeping neat scrapbooks of recipes and do-it-yourself tips

☺ Washing their cars at the weekend

☺ Masturbating

8 Unofficial Black Market Currencies of Turkey

🔲 Bribes

🔲 Black-market US dollars

🔲 Pretty young boys

🔲 Opiates

🔲 Squat-thrusts

🔲 Lambs sold into wool slavery

🔲 Second-hand copies of *All-Naked Bashi Bazouks*

🔲 Reach-arounds

12 Things Which Louis Armstrong Should Have Mentioned in 'What a Wonderful World' – But Didn't

✗ Oral sex

✗ Diet cola

✗ Powerful but gentle laxatives

✗ Kate Bush videos

✗ Anti-premature ejaculation creams

✕ Taramasalata

✕ Cadbury's

✕ Disneyland

✕ Easy credit

✕ Contraceptive devices

✕ Bank holidays

✕ Flushing toilets and toilet paper

15 Things Which Louis Armstrong Wouldn't Have Even Considered Mentioning in 'What a Wonderful World'

☛ Sudden death

☛ Hospital anaesthetists who get the gases mixed up and leave you with the IQ of a stick of parsley

☛ Martin Bormann

☛ Tonsillitis

☛ Old dogs with a chronic flatulence problem

☛ BO

☛ Difficult sums

☛ Scabby bits of your body

☛ The East German motor industry

☛ Income tax

☛ Commuting

☛ Perverts with your phone number

☛ Phone bills

☛ The Japanese

☛ Pot Noodles

DAY BY DAY

10 Stupid New Year's Resolutions

◆ Take up smoking

◆ Try and halve your salary

◆ Put on 84 lbs

◆ Breathe only once every 40 seconds

◆ Assassinate a foreign dignitary

◆ Put chocolate biscuits down your underwear every day for the whole year

◆ Sell your new car for £3.50

◆ Spend less time with your family

◆ Learn to recite the Koran in fluent Turkish

◆ Take this stupid book back to the shop

---

10 Stupid Advantages of Being 3 Feet Tall

☆ You can save money by wearing children's clothes (but then again, who wants to go through life wearing sailor outfits or blue velvet pinafore dresses with lace collars?)

☆ If a bullet was coming towards you 4 feet off the ground, it would miss you easily

☆ You're twice as tall as someone who's only 1' 6" tall

☆ You're a veritable giant amongst men compared with people who are only 1" tall

☆ You can headbutt bullies in the nuts

☆ You can look through keyholes without stooping

☆ You can get your identical twin to stand on your shoulders, cover yourselves with a long coat and get into an '18' film

☆ If you're destitute you need only a small cardboard box to live in

☆ If you're writing a dissertation on 'The Smell of People's Crotches', you're perfectly placed to do your research

☆ You're virtually guaranteed a part in *Snow White II: The Adventure Continues*

15 Things That Seem to Go on Forever

✖ Visits from relatives

✖ The Conservative Party's term in office

✖ Train journeys in carriages packed with drunken football fans

✖ Your time in the dentist's chair

✖ The wait between erections

✖ Exams you haven't revised for

✖ The wait before you get your exam results

✖ Your Barclaycard statement

✗ 20 consecutive 99-year prison sentences
✗ The trailers on a video before the main film starts
✗ Double maths lessons
✗ Correspondence with your insurance company
✗ Televised snooker tournaments
✗ Sexual intercourse with either one of the authors
✗ Infinity

9 Things That Always Seem to End Too Soon

☀ A ride on the dodgems
☀ An erection
☀ The latest episode of *The Simpsons*
☀ Your last relationship
☀ Sleep
☀ That pack of E-180 videos you bought
☀ Lunch breaks
☀ 15 minutes of fame
☀ Life

The 10 Least Popular Wallpaper Designs

▨ High-velocity bullet exit wound
▨ Fly on a windscreen
▨ Ruptured spleen
▨ Dead cat by the roadside
▨ Benito Mussolini's bottom
▨ Steaming turd

⬛ Interlocking swastikas
⬛ Burning orphans
⬛ TV interference
⬛ Red flock

---

10 Clues That Your Flatmate Might Be a Serial Killer

✕ He leaves the flat every night at 11 p.m. with an axe and comes back in the early hours of the morning, saying that he's 'been for a breath of fresh air'

✕ He's forever asking to borrow your blood Stain Devil

✕ He's always looking through the phone book and writing down names and addresses completely at random

✕ He changes his name by deed poll to 'Hannibal'

✕ He looks longingly at the skinned carcasses hanging in Dewhurst's window – even though he's a vegetarian

✕ He's always receiving brochures from surgical supply companies in the post

✕ His Black and Decker workmate is covered in what he claims is 'red paint'

✕ The scarf he wears looks suspiciously like a small intestine

✕ There's a naked leg sticking out from under his bed

✕ He's forever dragging things to the wheelie bin at the back of the flats in the dead of night

9 Stupid Things You'll Always Find in a Public Toilet

☛ A strategically placed spyhole through to the next cubicle

☛ Pervy and disgusting graffiti on the inside of the door that you feel compelled to read, even though you're repulsed

☛ A lone turd, floating

☛ Cheap toilet paper that's either abrasive or greasy

☛ Cigarette burns on the edge of the seat or on the top of the hot air dryers

☛ An unidentified substance on the handle that you discover by accident only when you come to flush

☛ A lock that doesn't

☛ A puddle of a strange, yet familiar-smelling liquid on the tiles

☛ Roller towels designed so that 78 people use the same 2-foot length of linen

10 Stupid Things You Won't Find in a Typical Amish Household

◆ A multiplay CD system and the whole set of Iron Maiden albums

◆ A huge poster of Freddy Krueger

◆ An Uzi

◆ Cocaine with a street value of $600,000

◆ The keys to a supercharged Pontiac Trans Am

◆ 27 back issues of *Playboy*, some with 'water damage'

◆ A wardrobe full of bright, skimpy beachwear

◆ A fridge crammed full of Buds

◆ Edible underwear

◆ A bottle of strawberry-flavoured 'Joy-Jelly'

16 Stupid Things That Secretaries Constantly Talk About

☆ Their boyfriend, Dave

☆ Anyone else called Dave

☆ Their ex-boyfriend

☆ Dave's ex-girlfriend

☆ Their hair

☆ Their clothes

☆ Dave's hair

☆ Dave's clothes

☆ Getting another job

☆ Mel Gibson

☆ Going to some club

☆ Going on holiday

☆ Their best friend

☆ Their best friend's hair

☆ Dave's job

☆ Any combination of any of the above

15 Stupid Things We Bet You've Always Wanted to Do

✗ Walk up a 'down' escalator

✗ Drive your car on purpose into the asshole who just cut you up

✗ Grope the person next to you on a crowded train

✗ Carry a big gun

✗ Answer a lonely hearts ad

✗ Hide in a department store and then wander around it alone after closing time

✗ Pose for a nudie mag

✗ Shoplift

✗ Kick a skinhead in the bollocks

✗ Join the 5-mile-high club

✗ Photocopy your bottom

✗ Measure your willie

✗ Have an affair

✗ Ask Debbie Greenwood for her autograph

✗ Tell the boss just what a wanker he really is

11 Stupid Things You Can Guarantee That Someone Called 'Darren' Will Do

☀ Think that white socks, Flintstone boxer shorts and a sovereign ring are the height of fashion

☀ Drive a knackered **XR**3i

☀ Act like a flash git half the time

☀ Act like a prat the rest of the time

- Talk utter crap all of the time
- Go on holiday wiv his mates
- Be nicknamed 'Daz' or 'Dazza'
- Go out with a peroxide blonde
- Live in some godforsaken part of Essex
- Anything dodgy
- Moonies

10 Stupid Things That Prove You're 'Well 'ard'

- Floss with barbed wire
- Drink 5 raw eggs and a bottle of Johnny Walker before breakfast
- Sing 'Sweet Child of Mine' at the top of your voice in the reference library
- Do a poo without washing your hands afterwards
- Do a poo without taking your trousers down beforehand
- At your wedding, when the vicar says 'Does anyone present object?', say, 'Yes, me' and then go home
- Wet shave with your eyes closed
- Punch a copper in the head for no apparent reason
- Punch yourself in the head for no apparent reason
- Yell, 'Whoo! Right through the head!' when Bambi's mother gets shot

What Your Best Friend Says (and What She Really Means)

✗ 'That look is really you.' (Cheap, uncoordinated and trashy)

✗ 'Of course it suits you.' (You always look that rough)

✗ 'I won't tell a soul, cross my heart.' (Where's my telephone book?)

✗ 'Of course it's not too small.' (You're just too large)

✗ 'Of course it's not too revealing.' (I can't wait to see their faces!)

✗ 'I wouldn't be telling you this if I weren't your friend.' (And didn't enjoy stirring it)

✗ 'Perhaps I shouldn't be telling you this . . .' (I can't wait to tell you this!)

✗ 'Maybe marriage will change him . . .' (I give the two of you six months, tops)

✗ 'No one will ever guess.' (Until I tell them, that is)

✗ 'You look fabulous!' (Tarty cow . . .)

✗ 'It's just what I've always wanted!' (You wait until your birthday . . .)

✗ 'Will you take a friendly word of advice . . .' (Or 20 minutes of calculated, vitriolic, malicious, catty criticism masquerading as advice?)

✗ 'Why don't you give him another chance?' (The last time was sooooo funny)

✗ 'You look like the perfect couple . . .' (Laurel and Hardy)

✕ 'Goodness knows what it must have cost
   you!' (£12.99 including VAT – which is
   half what I spent on you, you cow!)

✕ 'I just don't know how he found out.'
   (Unless me telling him had anything to
   do with it)

✕ 'I love those jeans on you.' (Because they
   accentuate your child-bearing hips)

✕ 'Everybody goes through it.' (If they're
   chronically plain and dull, that is . . .)

✕ 'That's the perfect dress for you!' (I can't
   be bothered to go back to all the other
   shops)

---

12 Unsuitable Topics of Conversation at a Dinner Party

☛ Rigor mortis

☛ Enemas

☛ The dog's boil

☛ Your boil

☛ Ethiopia

☛ Where that stuff between your toes comes
from

☛ How ugly the hostess is

☛ The art of Sam Peckinpah

☛ Where exactly the *vas deferens* is to be
found

☛ Your strange habit of spitting in any food
you cook

☛ Glass eyes

☛ The high local incidence of burglary when couples go out to dinner parties

28 Things You've Probably Got in Your Handbag Right This Very Minute

◆ A crumpled Danielle Steel paperback

◆ Some loose change

◆ Lipstick

◆ Make-up mirror

◆ A quarter of a packet of stale Polos

◆ A disposable lighter (empty)

◆ Hairspray

◆ A crumpled-up clipping from a problem page

◆ A crumpled-up, used Kleenex smeared with make-up

◆ A crumpled photo of your boyfriend

◆ A crumpled photo of your parents

◆ A powder compact

◆ A book of matches from a restaurant

◆ A phone number you jotted down, but can't remember whose

◆ A huge bunch of keys on a stupid novelty key ring

◆ Two unpaid bills

◆ Half an old chocolate bar covered with fluff

◆ Credit-card counterfoils

◆ The cap from an eyeliner pencil

◆ A nail file

◆ 1 stick of Juicy Fruit

◆ 3 loose tampons

◆ A dirty hairbrush

◆ Assorted receipts

◆ A purse

◆ A torn-out recipe you'll never make

◆ A diary you hardly ever use

◆ An old tangerine peel squashed down into one corner

8 Stupid Things to Do in the Clothes Shop

☆ Put all the size 10 dresses on size 14 hangers

☆ Ask the shop assistant if you can have a dress like hers, only two sizes smaller

☆ Wait until someone picks up a dress and heads for the changing room. Pick up an identical dress in the smallest size available and then follow her in. While she's undressing, swop the dresses over

☆ If someone asks you to do them up at the back, pretend to be violently struggling. Dig your knee into the small of her back and tug at the zip, puffing and panting. Say, 'I'll have to go and get a shoe horn' – and leave

☆ Ask the shop assistant for a dress like hers, only one that fits properly

☆ Find the most revolting dress in the entire shop and start enthusing about how trendy and exciting it is. Wait until the stampede for it starts and then slip out of the shop

☆ While someone is busy trying on a swimsuit, pick up all her discarded clothing, walk out, hand it to the assistant and say, 'No thanks. You can put them back now'

☆ When someone asks you to help them on with a dress, run a Stanley knife down the seam. Tell her to cross her arms to make sure it fits

18 Stupid and Heartless Things to Say in a Communal Changing Room

✗ That's a bit expensive just for a dare, isn't it?

✗ Excuse me, but have you seen the back of your knicks?

✗ I saw a dress just like that one in Woolworth's yesterday.

✗ Hey! Get out of here, you filthy pervert! Oh, I'm sorry. I thought you were a man. . . .

✗ I had a dress like that. My boyfriend made me throw it away because he said it made me look like Edna Everage

✗ Pardon me, but I think that will clash terribly with your spots. . . .

✗ Excuse me, but would you stop staring at me? Yes, *you*

✗ Look, if you're that desperate to attract a man I'll fix you up myself

- Excuse me for asking, but you seem to know something I don't. Is the 'plain, severe and drab' look in this season?
- I'd get some acne cream to go with that backless dress if I were you
- Size 12? That's a bit optimistic, isn't it?
- Hi, I'm from Weightwatchers
- I wouldn't buy that dress if I were you. All it does is accentuate your roots
- God. You'll have to shave those legs if you want to wear that . . .
- Excuse me, but since you're obviously colour blind would you like any help?
- Isn't it funny how some clothes just accentutate the tummy like that?
- God, you're fat. Don't you care about yourself?
- I'm sorry. I owe you an apology. I'm the store detective. I followed you in here because I thought you'd stuffed six dresses, four skirts and a raincoat up your jumper, but I can see now that it's really all you . . .

10 Things You *Really* Don't Want to See First Thing in the Morning

- That half-drained bottle of whisky from the night before
- The alarm clock telling you it's 10.30
- Yourself in the mirror
- Dried spew in your partner's hair (which

you know you'll have to tell them
about . . .)

☀ The washing-up you left in the sink, in
the hope that it would somehow do itself

☀ A big rip in the condom you dumped on
the bedside cabinet

☀ The remains of the Chinese takeaway all
over the coffee table

☀ Bonnie Langford plugging something on
TV-AM

☀ Yesterday's contraceptive pill, next to the
glass of water . . .

☀ What the dog did in the night . . .

10 Charities You'd Have to Be Stupid to Make Donations to

▪ Save the Cockroach

▪ The Shoot the Elderly Campaign

▪ The Distressed Nazi Gentlefolk
Association

▪ The Duchess of York's Appeal for better
skiing conditions in Klosters

▪ The Help the Rich and Privileged
Campaign

▪ Famine Relief for Switzerland

▪ Shotgun Aid (helping to keep blood sports
enthusiasts armed and ready!)

▪ Sponsored Giant Panda-Eating

▪ The Donate Your Kidneys to Rich Arabs
in Harley Street Clinics Appeal

▪ The Moonies

12 Things That Are More Expensive Than You Think

✗ A Feast ice lolly

✗ A cup of tea at the Ritz

✗ A return rail ticket to Liverpool

✗ Your car's 12,000-mile service

✗ Dental treatment

✗ A new pair of jeans

✗ 2 tickets to the theatre

✗ Having your shoes repaired

✗ A second-hand Volkswagen Golf

✗ A baby

✗ Living in London

✗ CDs

11 Stupid Things That People Suffering from Claustrophobia Shouldn't Really Do

☛ Travel by Underground

☛ Take up potholing

☛ Read the electricity meter under their stairs

☛ Buy a Fiat 126

☛ Buy a Fiat 126 and shut themselves in the boot

☛ Get buried alive

☛ Buy a Barratt starter home

☛ Buy a Barratt 2-bedroom flat

☛ Buy a Barratt 3-bedroom house

☞ Go up in a lift and deliberately jam it between floors

☞ Lock themselves in a wardrobe

10 Stupid Things They Don't Teach You at Finishing School

◆ How to get out of a Skoda Estelle without showing your knickers

◆ How to walk like an Egyptian

◆ How to blow the biggest bubbles with Juicy Fruit

◆ Interview techniques specifically geared towards placements at the Woolworth's Pick 'n' Mix counter

◆ How to pick your nose discreetly

◆ How to sign on

◆ How to shoplift at M & S

◆ How to speak like what Janet Street-Porter does

◆ How to make farty noises with your hand and armpit

◆ The Birdie Dance